A BRILLIANT IDEA EVERY

SECONDS...

Unlock Your Ideas and Creativity for
BUSINESS AND PERSONAL SUCCESS

MICHAEL KRYTON

"Michael Kryton has the unique ability to bring out the
creative genius inside us. His learnable techniques spawn
inspired solutions and can be tapped any time. Absolutely brilliant!"
—**Gary Chappell, Past President/CEO, Nightingale-Conant, Chicago**

A BRILLIANT IDEA EVERY 60 SECONDS

Unlock Your Ideas and Creativity for
Business and Personal Success

MICHAEL KRYTON

Published 2018 by Gildan Media LLC
aka G&D Media
www.GandDmedia.com

ISBN: 978-1-7225-0032-0

For those who inspire me.

My loving partner in life, my wife, my friend,

Jan

The Kryton Clan—Brock, Cole, Caleb, Hope, Suzanne, Alexis

My Mother, Father, and Sister, who I miss every day

My niece, Lisa Maria

My dear friends and colleagues

Who share my passion for creativity

Special thanks to Brilliant supporters.

Gary Chappell, Dan Strutzel, Shannon Berry, Terry Paranych, Mike Harding, Maria Laskar, Shiela Anderson,

Jeanine Laskar, Daryl Procinsky, Gilbert Allan, Chris Wait, Terry Grant

CONTENTS

A CREATIVE INTRODUCTION

Creativity is just connecting things. When you ask creative people how they did something, they feel a little guilty because they didn't really do it, they just saw something. It seemed obvious to them after a while. That's because they were able to connect experiences they've had and synthesize new things.
—Steve Jobs

Is it really possible to come up with a brilliant idea every 60 seconds? Reflecting on the perspective of Steve Jobs, the co-founder of Apple Inc., we can appreciate that creativity and ideation is more tangible than we realize. For me, it became a matter of professional survival.

Early in my career, I established a 60-second time challenge: to state a creative idea within the first 60 seconds of a meeting with a client, which would compel them to take me more seriously within the creative process. This powerful connection would eventually draw in all the other participants in any creative meeting and a different experience would unfold.

What kinds of ideas have the power to get this kind of attention? The answer to that question is the reason I wrote this book. It is not necessarily about the "Big Idea."

In fact, it's more about the *not*-so-big idea: the simple ideas by some standards, but, when examined closer, can yield incredible things. I think of them as *actionable* ideas.

Creativity is a big-basket word. What the world perceives as being creative, whether it is associated with art, science, music, advertising, fashion, writing, films, business, sports, politics, education—in fact, everything—is heavily influenced by the creative machines in such creative hubs as Hollywood, Silicon Valley, New York, Toronto, Vancouver, Montreal, London, Paris, Hong Kong . . . and even in my neck of the woods, Edmonton, Alberta.

Radio, television and the Internet also influence what we think a brilliant idea looks like. Films, TV programs, videos, radio programs, commercials, music, books, blogs,—they all take us somewhere, creatively. They shape our perception of what we think is creative and, by implication, what we think about our own creativity.

Ask someone on the street what he or she thinks is an example of creative thinking, and rarely does anyone say anything about an idea of their own. What do you think about your own creativity? Have you had a good idea lately? Would you know if you did?

I wish I had a quarter for every person who has ever said to me, "*I wish I could be as creative as you. How do you come up with ideas like that?*" The truth is, I don't really *come up* with ideas; I *find* them. Sometimes, they find me.

In the world of advertising where I honed my idea-generating process, the Big Idea was the prize everyone chased, and still does. Rather than climb creative mountains to reach the Big Idea, I decided to look for *actionable* ideas. It became a process that fueled the way I operate creatively. It rendered the notion of creativity, sometimes defined as a divinely prescribed gift, which we generally refer to as "talent," into something more relevant and on-the-street where most of us live and operate creatively.

An actionable idea is one that either helps us or inspires us to define the solutions we need; solutions to problems, titles, themes or slogans, solutions that allows us to articulate a process or procedure, concepts that inspire inventions or product innovations, solutions to improve relationships, strategic solutions . . . it is an endless list.

Actionable ideas are the derivatives of a string of ideas that come before it. We can produce several actionable ideas, all of which contribute to a solution. If we ever find a Big Idea, it owes its incarnation to the string of ideas that preceded it. You will learn more about "Idea Strings" (among several other things) and how every thought is part of an ongoing Idea String unravelling in our minds moment to moment.

We have ideas all the time, but we miss or overlook the brilliant ideas that flit through our minds even when they occur. Over the years, I learned to appreciate how ideas are connected and began to focus more on how a string of ideas is produced and how important every idea was to the process. Thomas Edison, the inventor of the light bulb, said, *"I have not failed. I've just found 10000 ways that won't work."* Adapting his thinking to mine, my belief is that a successful creative process produces many ideas leading to those which truly take us forward toward our objectives.

The objective of my methodology is to make the process of generating ideas more tangible for everyone. We tend to see ideas and creativity as something *out there.* You are probably familiar with the phrase "thinking outside the box." As much as I appreciate the analogy, I feel it positions ideation as something mythical. In my ideation about ideation (deliberate redundancy), there is nothing outside the box. We are always in a box of some kind, but we can make the box bigger, pushing the edges further out with every idea we generate. So, this is good news for everybody. We have ideas all the time and I am going to show you how to appreciate and harness the way you operate creatively.

In this book, ideas are interlaced throughout every chapter. The last chapter on case studies is devoted solely to ideas and concepts and you may be tempted to jump the cue. I encourage you to read *A Brilliant Idea Every 60 Seconds* from cover to cover. Or, if you decide to cut through the line and go to the last chapter pre-maturely, please return to your original place in the line-up of information afterwards. It will make much more sense to you in the end.

Before we get started, here are a few simple rules; truths really—creative truths.

A FEW CREATIVE TRUTHS: VOLUME I

---

1. There is no such thing as a stupid idea. I did not coin this rule. It is a universal proposition enforced by the creativity police everywhere. It was stolen from the public domain.

2. Only God, Allah, Buddha, Brahman—all capital 'C' Creators—actually *come up* with Big Ideas. I mean—I just don't have the qualifications to create a universe of reality driven by a time-continuum based on relativity.

3. Creativity is a thousand doors. Pick one.

4. Your children, mother, father, grandparents and favorite school teacher think you are creative. Are they wrong? On this rare occasion, they are right. As John Cleese said, *"Creativity is not a talent . . . It is a way of operating."*

5. The moment you yell, *"I'm such an idiot!"* and whack yourself on the side of your head, is a moment of pure, absolute creativity. The moment you start a sentence with, *"It occurred to me . . ."* is the moment your brain (while you weren't looking) connected some dots around something you've been thinking about and kicked it upstairs to your conscious mind where you found it.

6. Have you ever lied? The truth doesn't require creativity in the telling of it. Politicians sometimes legislate a version of truth and lawyers interpret it for the rest of us. That's a lot of creativity. Of course, we know that all kinds of people lie. Lying is hard work and requires a lot of creativity.

7. When you were a child, did you pretended to be someone else at Halloween. (Some of us still do.) You also turned an inanimate object into a weapon of destruction, transformed yourself into royalty with a handful of clothes, and managed to convince your parents that you were too sick to go to school. In some cases, you did this all on the same day.

8. Creativity is not exclusive to one person. It is a shared process, an ongoing collaboration that happens either by design or spontaneously.

9. Everyone is creative. People who say they are not creative are lying to themselves, and that's very creative.

10. Perfection is imperfection at work. Just as there is no such thing as a stupid idea, there is no such thing as a perfect idea.

PART 1.

CHAPTER 1.

THE ROAD TO BRILLIANT

Creativity is a great motivator because it makes people interested in what they are doing. Creativity gives hope that there can be a worthwhile idea. Creativity gives the possibility of some sort of achievement to everyone. Creativity makes life more fun and more interesting.
—Edward de Bono

Edward de Bono, physician, author (Six Thinking Hats) and inventor, coined the term "lateral thinking" in 1967, which is described as the process of solving problems through an indirect and creative approach, using reasoning that is not immediately obvious and involving ideas that may not be obtainable by using only traditional step-by-step logic. I didn't know about lateral thinking until recently, but it accurately describes my creative experience.

My entire life has been driven by creativity. I pursued any opportunity to try something new or test an idea. I started as a radio copywriter, a position I knew nothing about, but I was given an unexpected opportunity at a time when the requirements to get into the field were minimal—almost non-existent. If someone asked me about my capabilities to do something I had actually never done before, my answer was always an unflappable "*Yes!*" It was the only way I knew how to do things.

Even from the very beginning as a writer-producer-director working first in radio and later in all media, I had this propensity to run past myself. In the face of chaos and stress, my loosely defined mission to discover everything around creativity kept me moving forward. Inevitably, someone would say, "*Give up. It isn't going to work.*" Telling me that something wasn't worth doing (or trying) convinced me that it was worth examining, at least. And that was how I approached my first job as a copywriter in a small radio station in Northern Alberta.

Back then, radio copywriters or ad writers were not held in the highest regard. Over three decades later, not much has changed, sad to say. Copywriters are necessary cogs in the wheel because someone has to script and produce the ads for paying clients. The service (in radio) is free to the client, which further undermines any real value or consideration of creative skill. Unfortunately, most ad writers are not trained. The average radio copywriter understands little if nothing about activation methods, tone and manner—in other words, the technical aspects of writing ad copy. Neither did I when I started.

How I won my first national award within the first 6 months of writing and producing commercials is a function of imagination gone wild, unbridled and uninformed. The commercial that triggered it all was a funky rap I wrote and produced for a propane gas distributor. The acknowledgment was motivating. It also compelled me to *learn* about the craft; about marketing and advertising communications, and creative strategy—what activation methods and tone and manner were and how they worked.

However, there was nothing substantial in any form, which spoke to me about creative process, creative thinking, concept development and ideation. I relied only on my innate creative abilities. I did not *learn* to be creative or think creatively based on any particular educational process. Creativity was, for me, always there like an invisible friend. Eventually, I asked the question that launched my investigation: how do I generate ideas? How does anyone generate ideas and concepts? The other question was, why do many people say they don't have a creative bone in their body? This always baffled me.

Over the years, I worked with several clients who did not have faith in their own creativity. On top of that, they didn't have faith in radio copywriters either. Understandably, back then (latter '70s—early '80s), copywriters wrote by the seat of their IBM typewriter balls. Apart from a passing understanding of the importance of a good hook in a message, most copywriters relied on clichés to drive the message. At first, so did I.

You can still hear them today. *"Act now." "The Purrfect Pet Store wants you to know (fill in the blank)." "Hurry, this sale will end soon."* (And so will your career.) I realize I'm over-simplifying a smidge, but most veteran copywriters will understand the pith of what I'm pithing. It wasn't that writers didn't generate interesting ideas and concepts, it was the execution, which would unravel the best creative intentions.

I didn't want to be one of those writers. I wanted to know how and why the creative process worked. So I tried to educate myself. Having read a few simple books relating to marketing communications and advertising, I developed a layman's understanding of how creativity served a business function. Creating commercials wasn't just about the written or spoken expression of ideas. It was much more than that.

It was a process connected to defining who the audience was, the position of the brand in the marketplace, the unique selling proposition (USP), the way radio actually worked as a medium and the nagging fact that radio commercials were *heard* but not really *listened* to. Commercials were annoying; they still are for the most part. For me, it was like working in a vacuum where no one can hear you scream.

Speaking of screaming. In those days, *hard sell* commercials reigned supreme. We engaged in barking and yelling at the target audience because, as many clients repeated over and over *ad nauseum,* this would be the way to get the masses' attention. Yelling in a library will get attention, too, but, it didn't mean anyone would actually hear anything of value or remember the message. For me, getting attention was becoming an art and science.

I liked using radio as a canvas, engaging the theatre-of-the-mind to position thoughts and ideas in people's heads. Granted, most of the time, it was about making a purchase. Nonetheless, the objective was to create commercials that would creep into the mind via the ear with strategic stealth. I talked to my clients about "purchasing behavior" and "consumer psychology," waxing eloquently about "activation methods" such as "motivation through psychological appeal"—blah blah blah as it was known to them.

Salespeople would advise me (nag me, really) to just give the client what they want, to which my response was that what the client really *wants* is an ad campaign that actually works. Research backed me up. Consumers didn't believe 85 percent of the things communicated in advertising regardless of the medium, especially commercials that asserted notions such as, *"the customer is number one."* My point was that squawking among the many other squawkers on the air wouldn't do anything to generate results.

With all the knowledge I was accumulating about advertising communication, I was missing the mark. It wasn't just art and science. It was about how we think, work and operate creatively. As I began to wrap my mind around this idea, I realized I had to change the way I was operating with clients. The one thing I changed in my creative process came out of desperation. It evolved organically and out of necessity.

Simply put, I took every opportunity in a meeting with any client, especially new ones, to express an idea within the first 60 seconds—any idea or concept that would rattle their creative chain. It didn't matter whether the idea would see the light of day. Somehow, I was able to do it consistently. The response from clients was usually positive and it didn't matter if they committed to the idea. All that mattered is that they liked the idea and, hopefully, liked me and, more importantly, respected my creative ability.

My approach turned these creative discussions into a creative collaboration, something I would understand more about as the years went on. Critical to that understanding would be my sense, perhaps empathetic, of their quest to find a good idea—a brilliant idea. Bill Gates once said, *"At Microsoft there are lots of brilliant ideas but the image is that they all come from the top—I'm afraid that's not quite right."* As he suggested, brilliant ideas are given life by everyone—even clients.

As my techniques developed, I used them to negotiate the creative process and advance what I thought were the stronger concepts and ideas, regardless of who the author was, leading to the drafting of scripts and finally producing them into existence.

Most of these campaigns actually worked. Clients were receiving positive feedback from customers on their commercials. The campaigns were producing tangible results. Increased traffic in the store and sales at the till were the proof of the pudding. My creative reputation gained ground steadily. Within a couple of years, I was working with everyone from retail clients to elected officials. No matter who I worked for, I wanted it to work—period. It was an obsession. Still is.

When I was awarded a citation from the Hollywood Radio & Television Society recognizing a commercial I wrote and produced for Nutrisystem as an example of one of the "World's Best Broadcast Advertisements," I figured I knew what I was doing. The reality was, I had barely scratched the surface. The process of generating ideas within the first 60 seconds of a creative discussion was driving a career, but I realized I was limited by the fact that I could not answer the one question people kept asking me: *how* do you do it? It was a nagging chorus and it irked me that I couldn't respond to it. Then, a simple conversation turned into a tipping point.

I was having a discussion with a colleague about a *"Unique Selling Proposition"* (USP). In advertising communication, a Unique Selling Proposition is the expression of a key value or quality of a product that differentiates itself from any other similar product. What makes it unique or exclusive? The USP will tell you. Here is one historic example of a classic USP.

- Dominos Pizza:
  "You get fresh, hot pizza delivered to your door in 30 minutes or less or it's free."

As we struggled to define the USP of a particular client, I kept coming back to the question, what actually is the inherent value? How do we define them? The discussion continued at length as we tried to articulate the inherent values hiding in our creative assignments.

It was my assertion that the relationship between a product and user was driven by an inherent value. For example, the *function* of a product was an inherent value. That was just the beginning. I realized that there were many more inherent values. It crystallized the creative process for me in a way that would drive it to this very day.

For years, I referred to inherent values in my creative discussions with clients and colleagues. Interestingly enough, years later, I noticed marketing textbooks referring to "inherent *qualities*" when describing the key factors which define a marketing and advertising campaign. Notwithstanding the academic context of inherent value, academia still did not connect inherent value to the creative process in a tangible way. In other words, in academia, inherent value was approached intellectually and in a more limited fashion.

My application of inherent value was becoming a hunting expedition in a universe of creative possibilities, a quest that reached beyond the world of advertising. I wanted to develop a tangible, on-the-street, working guide—a tool kit of creative mechanics—which anyone could use to generate actionable ideas quickly. I have always believed that everyone is creative and, with a little guidance, can grow their creative potential given the right tools.

William Shatner said, *"Given the freedom to create, everybody is creative. All of us have an innate, instinctive desire to change our environment, to put our original stamp on this world, to tell a story never told before. I'm absolutely thrilled at the moment of creativity—when suddenly I've synthesized my experiences, reality, and my imagination into something entirely new. But most people are too busy working on survival to find the opportunity to create."*

When I was asked to co-script and direct *"How Time Flies,"* William Shatner's Canadian live show tour in 2011, I knew my creative methodology would be put to the ultimate test. I also knew that Mr. Shatner would have his own creative process. The question was, would my approach work in sync with his? Well, destiny gave me a chance to find out.

I first met Mr. Shatner in Los Angeles. Here he was, the iconic figure, an actor who had reinvented his career several times, appearing in the most celebrated productions on television, in film, on the Canadian theatre stage and on Broadway. At 82, he was still as spry creatively as anyone in our industry could hope to be at that stage of life.

Going into the creative process with Mr. Shatner, I felt confident I would be able to connect well with him and establish a creative relationship based on give and take. I reminded myself that this was still like many other meetings: get to know the client and throw out an idea within 60 seconds. That's exactly what happened. And it worked, as it always had. Later in the book, I will share more of my star-struck trek with the man.

What I have learned after three and half decades of practice is that the learning never stops. As I have continued to share my methodology on idea generation, it has come back to me through the new understandings and perspectives of others, confirming my belief that everyone can learn to generate actionable ideas quickly. It is a completely tangible, creative experience to be realized by everyone.

CHAPTER 2.

THE SOCIETY OF GREAT CREATORS

Do you want to know what you are? You are a creator. At every moment you are creating. The real question is, what are you creating?
—Bryant H. McGill

American author, Bryant McGill (Voice of Reason), echoes my belief that we are all creators. It is a given as far as I'm concerned; however, many choose to either ignore their creativity or play it down through comparison to others who are celebrated as being very creative. That kind of thinking is unfortunate, almost sad, because it prevents well-intentioned human beings from taking responsibility for the many things, good and bad, which happen in their lives.

Creativity is, in part, a gift in our lives from whoever or whatever created the universe—or created creativity—or created the creator. And so, I present the early icons of the creative complex.

Hinduism holds that Brahman is the foundation of all being, and that the universe has a definite origin from Brahman. In Christianity and Judaism, God is the Creator of all things. Allah, the God of Islam is the creator of the universe and everything in it, including all its cause and effect relationships.

Then, of course, there's Darwin, the nineteenth century English biologist, who is vague on creation and more remembered for his explanation of natural selection, which forms the spine of his concept about evolution. But, if we are to take anything from his thinking, it is that birds, lizards and insects are very interesting in terms of their creativity applied to survival.

Last, but not least, is the mighty Arkleseizure. He sneezed the universe out of his nose according to the "Hitchhiker's Guide to the Galaxy." So much for the Great Creator. I promise, we will not be banging the universe into existence and, as for that sneeze, there are plenty of nose wipes to go around.

Except for Darwin who, technically, is not a Creator, but more of a voice trying to explain creation in the wilderness, all the other Creators relied on scribes to document their creativity. In your life, have you ever documented your own creativity? If you wrote a diary, performed in front of a camcorder, wrote an essay, drew a picture, or at any moment said, *"Wait, I have an idea!"* you immediately qualified as a member of the Society of Great Creators.

All that to say you can come up with a brilliant idea in 60 seconds—maybe not a universe with a perfectly chaotic, random, time-continuum; but, ideas that work. You may not think you know how yet—or—how to do it better. The fact is, you already know how; some of you just don't remember. My job is to jog your memory.

CHAPTER 3.

THE SOCIETY OF DECREATORS

Evil being the root of mystery, pain is the root of knowledge.
—Simone Weil

French philosopher, Simone Weil, described decreation as *"undoing the creature in us"*–an undoing of self. Heaven and hell. God and the devil. Good and evil. Love and hate. Right and wrong. North Pole and South Pole. Creation and destruction. Perfection and imperfection. Giving in and giving up. Positive and negative. Impossible—*I'm possible.*

Polarization, in the scientific context, is about the balance of nature. Without some of these natural laws, chaos would reign supreme, although chaos still has to be factored in. What exactly is chaos? The "chaos theory" is what scientists use to describe disorder, but it is really about finding order in the random data.

One has to admire the human intellect and its determination to make order out of disorder. If anything, our quest to do so reveals our connection to polarization. When I am overwhelmed with decision-making, life changing circumstances, or any kind of challenge to a sense of balance, I often choose to shift into a less polarized state that might be referred to as 'gray.' I am often criticized for my *black and white* thinking. It is disconcerting to me when I am perceived as someone who does not embrace the *gray*—because I do. Don't we all on some level? But, really, what is this thing called "gray"?

"Gray" refers to a realm of thinking within which we often let denial or wishful thinking, among other things, influence our actions. It is where vague commitments are made; safe commitments that don't really mean anything and where we live in our stories about what happened in our lives, rather than understanding exactly what happened and moving on.

It is safer to be wishy-washy, so, we hide in the gray from the black and white, trying to escape and hide from the things that would otherwise motivate or provoke us to make commitments and take action. As a result, the creative process can slowly suffocate.

We bury our creative nature in the quagmire of our circumstances, arriving at the conclusion that we have nothing creative to offer; that we can't change anything or make a difference. When someone says, *"I'm not creative."*—or—*"I don't have any good ideas."*—I know they have wandered into the gray spectrum. Exercising creativity requires us to take risks. Too many of us choose not to take them. It's not that we *can't* be creative; rather, we *choose* to limit ourselves. But there are worse things. Where the gray thinking can limit creativity, decreation kills it.

Decreation is invoked by the person who says in a meeting, *"We need good ideas.,"* or, *"We need to think outside the box."* For those in the meeting who don't believe they are very creative, they remain silent for the duration of it. If anyone has the courage to say anything, it often comes in the form of limp support for an idea that appears *safe*—in other words, *gray.*

The safe idea has the best chance to be accepted by the person in control. Once they validate it, the assembled group conforms to its acceptance. Too often, it's about pleasing someone in power. Think of the politician who keeps saying, *"It's a gray area."* The minions and protégées around this person usually do not feel free enough to express themselves creatively. They are safer as a chorus. Consensus is like a bland salad dressing. Committees can be lethal to creativity.

In a speech at a business conference in Edmonton given by Elyse Allan, President and CEO of GE Canada, she clearly placed an emphasis on the need in the business sector for innovative thinking and that corporations needed to create a more open environment committed to fostering creative thinking. Bravo! And good luck with that.

Some creative professionals (like ad writers, creative directors, directors of communication, etc.) learn the art of persuasion, convincing a client that an idea the client did not initiate is an idea they did come up with. Making them think it is their idea is a somewhat gratuitous act, but a matter of necessity and survival for creative professionals. As a creative professional, I am guilty of doing this to advance a creative process, but, I am more interested in the idea itself rather than who gets the credit for it.

The process of decreation occurs in many situations. In a family, parents will invalidate a child's ideas (unknowingly usually) and undermine their creative disposition. When a parent does not acknowledge a child's creative experience (the child's signal being, *"Look at what I did."*), it can have consequences. The lack of acknowledgment adversely affects the creative identity of a child just as much as negative criticism.

My father had a hard time accepting my predisposition to play rock and roll music on the piano (Elton John; Emerson, Lake and Palmer; Leon Russell). His concept around my musical interests was for me to become a concert pianist. Never happened. And we had serious debates over the issue. Creatively, I never wavered. Unfortunately, my father never really understood my decisions creatively or professionally. Nonetheless, I don't regret my choices.

Sadly, he missed out on many things that were worthwhile as creative experiences we could have shared. He never heard many of the musical pieces I composed that were not rock in style but were, in fact, very classical. He never heard my commercial jingles or the music I composed or performed for television programming.

Fast forward many years later. After high school, my eldest son enrolled in university pursuing sciences and imploded by the end of the first semester. At that point, I said to him, *"Creativity is a thousand doors. Pick one."*

So, he bought a camera and, before long, was working professionally. Later, he enrolled in a photography and design program. He graduated at the top of his class three years later, all the while working professionally for prestigious corporate clients. He is now a brilliant photographer, designer and creative thinker.

The sad truth is that many parents will suffocate their children's creative potential, bending them to fulfill their own limited concept of what is right or expected, especially when it comes to being creative.

Decreation is how we ignorantly or, sometimes, deliberately impose our selfish creative will on others and, by doing so, shut down the creative process altogether. Creativity is a *shared* process. Anything that violates the positive sharing of creativity is decreation. What are you creating? What are you decreating? Who is it affecting? Are you selfishly creating barriers or selflessly promoting opportunities?

In a situation, discussion, meeting, or think tank focused on generating ideas, have you ever said or heard anyone say:

- *"That's a stupid idea."*
- *"That's a weak idea"*
- *"I don't think that's going to work."*
- *"That's not really what we're looking for."*
- *"We need something bigger."*
- *"Not sure about that idea."*
- *"We have to start thinking outside the box, people."*

Well, I'm confident and excited about every idea. What about you? What do you do in a creative think tank? What do others do that undermine or inspire your own creative potential? I recognize that you may not be aware of what it is that limits your creativity in general, whether it is at your own hand or due to the actions of the people around you. Much of what bridles your creativity probably has its origins in how others treated you or responded to you in situations where you were expressing your creativity.

Whatever your history is, your creative nature is always within you. It may be in mothballs, but it is still there. Just telling you this means very little. My purpose is to restore and unleash the creative person inside you. For those of you who are already free creatively, my purpose is to help you enhance what you already have. Okay, group hug. Moving on.

CHAPTER 4.

"I'M NOT CREATIVE AT ALL"

Creativity takes courage.
—Henri Matisse

Artists like Matisse, the great French painter, took risks. His contemporary, Picasso, was even more daring and controversial. Their art influenced abstract visual thinking and swept in a new genre. Well, I am not Matisse, Picasso, Thomas Edison, Richard Branson, Stephen Jobs, or Steven Spielberg. But I do have a sense of what it feels like to sum up the courage to pursue an idea.

Everyone needs an idea: concepts for innovation, solutions to problems, USPs for advertising campaigns, slogans for businesses and organizations, themes for annual general meetings, graduations and birthday parties, names for products, brands, babies and boats, script ideas for movies and commercials, words and messages for notes, memos and cards, lyrics, email messages, invitations . . . anything that involves a brush, pen, keyboard, microphone, camera, spoken word—or whatever form it is in which we transcribe our ideas within a creative manifestation.

The agenda might be focused on a process. For example, you may be looking for ideas relating to professional objectives concerning design, best practices, administration or management. As a coach, you might need ideas that could impact your team's performance. On a personal or professional level, you might be looking for ideas that could help improve relationships or improve your health. We are always looking for ideas. Actionable ideas.

As I stated earlier, I wish I had a dollar for every person I have met who said, *"I'm not creative at all."* OR—*"You are a very creative person, but I can't do what you do at your level."* Well—*yes*—you can! Although I believe everyone is creative, I understand why many people think otherwise. My mission is to change that kind of thinking or, at the very least, redirect it.

The creative experience is something that we are not always aware of, which means that an individual may think or do something creative—in fact, *very* creative—but does not recognize how creative it is and the impact it has on others and the process they're engaged in.

Side step for a moment. A little exercise. Take a few moments to remember when, in, say, the last two or three weeks, you had a moment when you thought or started to say, *"Something just occurred to me."* To repeat the Creative Truth I shared with you earlier, when that happens, your brain, without you looking, connected some dots around something you were thinking about, and kicked it upstairs to your conscious mind where you found it. You will see that statement a few times in this book, especially in the last chapter, Case Studies. On the surface, it may appear that I skipped a step, but I haven't. But, I'm beginning to jump the gun.

Back to where we were. Many people I have talked to equate creativity with a beautiful painting, an actor's performance, a writer's deft manipulation of characters and plot in a novel, a motivated speaker who captivates an audience, or a child who invents a world using a handful of figurines and props. Many people wonder how they come up with their ideas. Well, how *do* they generate ideas and concepts?

Painters, sculptors and photographers look for visual ideas. Musicians and songwriters listen to the silence hoping to hear an idea that will fill it. Writers stare at blank pages in the quest to find the words that will tell the story, express the sentiment or frame the argument. Create your own list of what you think creativity looks like. What do you know about the way in which you generate ideas?

On some level, most people deny their own creativity; however, self-denial is one of the most complex, creative acts we carry out on a daily basis. The amount of thought it takes to deflect one's own creativity—or anything else for that matter—is truly astounding. It is a conundrum of sorts. As we search for ideas—brilliant ideas—we deny that we have the creative ability to find them.

My objective is to help you open new doors and explore, develop and enhance your creative abilities and imagination, such that you can find actionable ideas quickly. The first step is to understand the *nature* of your creativity and your creative intelligence. Like emotional intelligence, creative intelligence can be developed. No matter how you view or understand creativity, especially your own creativity, there is always an opportunity to learn more.

A good friend of mine, Terry Paranych, now considered the go-to real estate expert in Canada, parlayed his way to one of the most successful real estate careers by trying everything. And I mean everything from wearing Superman outfits to creating a real estate marketing system that is being adopted by agents everywhere. Despite limited education, a fact he is candid about, he learned by trying things. Not everything worked, but the things that did work propelled a very interesting career. His message has always been the same. *"Don't give up, no matter what."*

Inside you is a creative person who can generate a brilliant idea in 60 seconds. Let's try to find or rediscover that creative power and see what happens. Whatever you do, the only thing I ask is, don't give up. Ready to play?

PART 2.

CHAPTER 5.

THE NATURE OF OUR CREATIVITY

Life's like a movie, write your own ending. Keep believing, keep pretending.
—Jim Henson

What's your story? Everyone has a story—many stories, some of which were authored in childhood. Then, we grow up and when we talk about ourselves, we dip into the vault of stories, which continue to evolve and develop, chapter by chapter. The stories are endless: the first time something bad happened in our lives; the first rejection from someone we loved; the most embarrassing moment; the first, significant triumph over challenge or adversity.

I owe my appreciation of storytelling to Drew Martin, a producer, director and writer I worked with at the Idea Factory, a television production company in Edmonton. He was always dedicated to the story, regardless of the context: commercial, documentary, feature film or corporate video. He said to me often, *"Follow the story."* It became a significant part of my creative process.

In some ways, we become the puppet we control through our own stories, manipulating the memory of reality with the skill of a Jim Henson, the master puppeteer and creator of Kermit the Frog. We keep writing and rewriting the stories in our heads, sometimes to the point that what actually happened in the first place becomes so transformed or obfuscated that, eventually, the event and the story are no longer the same. Despite the fact that we smudge, blur and alter the past (which is actually quite creative), can we, as Henson suggests, write our own ending?

A little history always hurts or humbles. Your own history has left powerful implants that are hard wired to your imagination. How did your history affect your own creativity? The idea here is to understand it and, by doing so, change it or enhance it. Resurrect it perhaps. Improve it. Definitely unleash it.

A little street-smart psychology. A child's creativity from the time they are born to about age 5 is, at once, both natural and influenced. Our sense of creativity is shaped and affected by Mom and Dad, siblings, as well as the pre-school environment and the first friends in life. There are other influences, but there are books out there that flesh it out with authority.

After the 5th year, things really change. We begin to remember more of what we see and hear. Our values develop and guide our thinking, feeling and imagination. More importantly, we begin to make more defined, creative choices.

Our first, substantive, creative experiences happen when we play or pretend as children. In other words, as toddlers, we start to move from playing randomly with something designed for a simple purpose—such as shaking a noise maker or grabbing something and winging it across the room—to creating simple stories using toys or props—and people.

Within those stories, we became something: a character or simply the force behind the manifestation, such as the hand that moves a racing car or the hand that animates the doll and the voice that speaks its thoughts. Of course, at that early stage in life, we don't suddenly stop and say, *"Gee, I'm creative."* It comes out more as, *"Look at what I did with Sparky, Mom."* And it is Mom who, after savouring the image of Sparky dressed as the big bad wolf and strapped to a toy stroller, will say, *"Gee honey, that's very creative."* But for a child, that's not the point.

The truth is, the child won't understand what Mom meant. What the child wants to hear is, *"Wow, Sparky looks like the big bad wolf. Well done!"* For children, it's about the result and the pat on the back; it's about validation on several levels. But, hey, I'm a writer, not Freud.

Pretending is a powerful activity because it invites us to freely interact with our imagination. Ideas are fluid and constant. Pretending constitutes almost every aspect of creativity: storytelling, role play, and the manipulation of environments and objects. It feeds off of our imagination and psychology. We transform, bend and manufacture new realities while suspending some of those belief systems and values, which would otherwise limit us. When we pretend, we release our creativity and allow it to operate. It is the nuclear reactor of idea generation.

Sadly, many of us forget to pretend as we grow up. It is time you were reminded. Now is the moment to reactivate your creativity—and have fun.

CHAPTER 6.

THE SIX QUESTIONS

What were the pretending stories or scenarios about?

There are six key questions I ask an individual about their creative experience as a child, which helps them get more in touch with their creative nature and imagination.

1. When you were a child, what activities did you engage in which involved pretending? In other words, how did you express your imagination?

2. What were the stories or scenarios about?

3. Where were you when you engaged in those activities?

4. What props and materials were involved?

5. Were you alone or were others involved?

6. What role did everyone (including you) play?

Although these questions apply to childhood, they can also be applied to adolescent and adult experiences. As an adult, I have always imagined myself being interviewed by Oprah Winfrey. The subject? *Creativity,* of course. Earl Nightingale, the legendary speaker and author of *The Strangest Secret,* said, *"We become what we think about."*

WHAT "PRETENDING" ACTIVITIES DID YOU ENGAGE IN AS A CHILD?

I spent a lot of time alone as a child. My sister, Lilian, was eight years older than I and, although we did play together for a time in our youth, I often found myself left to my own devices when it came to finding something to do. For whatever reason, my imagination drove my childhood experiences in a way that prevails to this day. When I connect the dots back to my childhood (an idea inspired by Stephen Jobs), it isn't hard to see how cause and effect worked in my life.

My Father was old enough to be my grandfather. That reality somehow connected me to World War 2, and, as a child at the summer cabin (from 8 to 11 years of age), I loved to grab an old army back pack, his British army beret and my Daisy air rifle, and equip myself with oddly shaped, non descript machine parts, which doubled as grenades and radios. Costume and props in hand, I would head out into the fields and search out the enemy, embarking on a mission that was destined to be a story of adventure and triumph.

My troop went on several missions. Curiously, we spent more time searching for the enemy and rarely engaging in the actual battle. But the storyline carried me over miles of territory and filled hours of time. For me, it was more about the process than the result. If there was any result, it was the satisfaction I gleaned from the event itself. But I valued the time hunting through the fields and deep woods, hiding behind trees, climbing them, burying myself in high grass, tracing the river next to the sand pit and surveying the panoramic vistas and horizons of the Eastern Townships south of Montreal where I spent many childhood summers.

I was always the leader of the troop, and, by all accounts, my men respected and trusted me. I never had to discipline anyone under my command. And no one ever died; a perfect, harmless war. Those experiences in the wind-swept fields imbued me with something that motivated my life's creativity. I was a storyteller who loved the unfolding plot more than the climax. At the heart of my creative experience was the love for the process. Other significant events contributed to the development of my creative nature.

When I was ten, Santa brought me a tape recorder and a sound effects record. Suddenly, I was producing dramatic radio shows. What was really quite curious is how I inserted commercials between scenes. The storyteller had become a producer. And the rest, as they say, is history.

Enough about me. What about you?

Did you play hockey, football, baseball or any other sport? Did you play on your own, play with others, or both? Which hero did you invoke to score the last goal, touchdown or home run? How many times did you win an imaginary championship or save the day?

What stories did you create? Was there a beginning, middle and end to those stories? Or was it just a process—in other words—was it about the story in the moment? Was it planned or spontaneous? Was it hands on and driven by your props or figures? Was there dialogue or narrative? Was it the same story every time or a mini-series?

Certainly, you found yourself unleashing your imagination in a variety of ways. It is an interesting exercise to reflect on the scenarios that you created out of your imagination. Most likely, you engaged in some stories more frequently than others. But all of them connect to your creativity today in some way. The challenge is to find the connection—again. Sometimes, it's very obvious, but not always.

WHAT WERE THE PRETENDING STORIES OR SCENARIOS ABOUT?

To some degree, I just covered this, but it bears further investigation. From the time in our history when human beings were able to communicate on some level, we have been story tellers. It is how we passed on knowledge and experience, celebrated our triumphs, lamented our tragedies, and paid homage to some greater entity in the universe.

Everyday, we tell stories. In fact, when we look at the

endless stream of Facebook postings (and other social media channels), we can see the diary of the human condition unfolding every second. At this writing, over 700 million active Facebook users post 17 billion located-tagged posts according to the DMR Digital Marketing Solutions website. Although there is a growing number of social media users under the age of 17 (5% of the total as stated by Pingdom), children under the age of 10 still engage in games of pretending. Enough statistics.

The process of pretending is an act of storytelling. The stories may be fragmented, jumping freely from one aspect to another. Children will cut to the chase whenever they are so inclined. If an idea occurs to them, they often act on it right away. As we grow older, the filters build up and we are more inclined to over analyze things, which often bogs us down creatively. But what is so important about storytelling?

Stories help us to create a context. Children don't analyze or rationalize this. Their stories are simple, generally speaking, but they organically develop their stories into a game of pretending that can become very complex. As a young child, my daughter, Hope, would assemble dozens of stuffed animals within a very well appointed classroom and teach them about everything from food to language. The classroom set-up, with easels, tables, chairs and wall mounted posters, took more time to assemble than the actual act of teaching, which, in and of itself, tells a story about my daughter's creativity. She is now very involved with drama studies in school and loves working backstage as much as she enjoys acting.

An exercise. Take a few minutes and write down the stories you remember engaging in as a child, which formed the basis of your games of pretending. Once you have your list, categorize them according to context. There may be several contexts or you may find they all share a similar one. Following are some of these contexts.

Plot driven. Christopher Booker, author of *The 7 Basic Plots*, divides storytelling into 7 basic story archetypes, which are:

- **Overcoming the Monster**
- **Rags to Riches**
- **The Quest**
- **Voyage and Return**
- **Comedy**
- **Tragedy**
- **Rebirth**

Fragments of life. This is a context of my own invention. These stories are more about relationships and processes without the stories having a particular plot or destination. These include:

- Tea parties
- Teaching
- Performing, such as dancing, putting on a variety show or playing rock star

Attitudes of life. Another one of my inventions. This

is where we pontificate, lecture, explain, imagine we are a celebrated speaker addressing loyal fans, a pastor preaching to his flock, or a star being interviewed about his fabulous life. This will inspire such things as:

- Monologues
- Speeches
- Talk shows or media interviews
- Conversations with invisible friends or aliens, depending in which universe your story is happening

Certainly, there is crossover. Conversations with invisible friends can take place during a tea party. A monologue might be a part of any of the plot-driven stories mentioned earlier. These contexts follow us throughout our life of storytelling. When you begin to recognize the contexts that you connect to, you can begin to connect more deeply with your creativity. The fact is, most of us don't take the time to make the connection or explore it. In other words, we take storytelling for granted.

The moment you are motivated or compelled to tell a story in response to something someone says, you have evidence of your creativity at work. The spark that occurs in that moment is the same spark that drives your creative ability to generate ideas.

I would add that you don't have to be the most eloquent storyteller to access a deeper understanding of your creative thinking process. Ideas are fragments of imagination. One word or one visual can inspire many ideas. There is no requirement to be an artist or a genius. In fact, artists and geniuses struggle just as much as anyone else with the process of ideation.

WHERE WERE YOU WHEN YOU ENGAGED IN THOSE PRETENDING ACTIVITIES?

Places and spaces have more impact on our inspiration and imagination than we realize. What is more telling about our own creativity is how we manifest different places and spaces in those environments. Backyard hockey rinks become legendary arenas. A carpet pattern becomes a roadway. A dollhouse becomes a home. A workbench or kitchen is transformed into a laboratory for a nurse, doctor and inventor, mad or otherwise. We turn sheds into forts. The patio deck and lawn set the stage for the next epic sea battle to be played out on the HMS Imagination. The computer desk and screen become the command centre for the next interstellar space voyage.

In today's world of proliferating electronic games and computer applications, it is disconcerting to watch our children become attached to the imaginary, virtual worlds created by skilled designers and programmers. It is a conundrum for me. At once, I respect the creativity of the programmers and, yet, as a parent, I feel angst about the impact the computer and video games are having on young minds—and not-so-young minds. It is a quandary begging for a creative solution. Or, on the other hand, let the evolution continue and we will learn from it. My objective has been to tear my children away from those worlds from time to time and they still enjoy creativity in a non-electronic environment just as much.

As a child, the worlds I created within what nature handed me were very important. Hills and rivers stimulated me. The geometry of architecture fascinated me and challenged my imagination. Perspectives and vanishing points attracted my eye and lured my creative spirit. To this day, the quality of the space around me is critical to my creative process.

It has made me wonder how others are affected by the moods and feelings inspired by walls, dividers, forests, job sites, cubicles, aisles, corner offices with large windows, and basement dens with no windows. Wherever my works takes me, I study the environments others toil in and I am both humbled and educated when I compare their working situation to mine. What I find is that the attitudes of the people within those spaces and places are linked to their surroundings.

For example, the "cuber" (those who work in cubicles) is often regimented, anal and resistant to the challenge of fully participating in creative processes. That is because he or she works in a very limited box. As I stated earlier, there always is a box. It is easier to understand the concept of a bigger box than it is to accept the notion of standing on an invisible ledge outside of it. But department heads, goaded by their executives, persist in asking their staff to stand on the ledge. Speaking of executives . . .

The corner office executive feels anointed with a sense of power and limitless potential—but often really feels cornered, outflanked by office politics, especially at the executive level. The park ranger is both mellow and gritty. The doctor and nurse are sterile, yet caring. The job site is under construction, much like the construction workers. The school classroom tells a character story. A confused room reveals a scattered teacher commanding students in chaos. A pristine room reflects the regimentation of a highly organized instructor with students and minds lined up for productivity. I realize these are all sweeping generalizations, but I have met and worked with these kinds of people many times. (Not all nurses and doctors are sterile.)

If you were to follow the trail of your memories back to the rooms (inside or outside) of your life, what would you discover about the connection to them in your current situation? Did you try to replicate the summer home you enjoyed as a child? Do you watch the world silently from your perch in a high-rise? Do you stare aimlessly at the sky and the clouds imagining what could have been or what might be? Do you lie back in a field and stare at the stars wondering about everything while counting the satellites? Is water nearby? Are you surrounded by mountains and hills or brick and mortar?

How does light affect you? Is it semi-opaque sheers that cover your windows—or do blinds and thick drapes hide the sun and streetlights? Is your deck your sanctuary? Is it a room you need to be in so that you can think or reflect? Or do you need to walk a path to find your opinions or ideas? The space around you is not the final frontier. It is, however, where you can discover the universe of your imagination.

WHAT PROPS AND MATERIALS WERE INVOLVED?

A sofa becomes a drum set. As a youngster, I used to

beat the crap out of our sofa in the recreation room with drum sticks releasing endless clouds of dust. My mom was not so impressed.

My dad was an architect. Our basement was filled with a plethora of building material samples he brought home regularly; anything from pieces of mosaic and fixtures to carved pieces of wood. And then, there was the paper log pile of rolled up blueprints. Altogether, it was the springboard for the stories I created about a mad inventor. Rainy days were never a problem.

When my father handed me a chrome, light meter, something he never really used when taking photographs, I drooled over it. It was saddled in a deep-brown, leather case and, for the first hour, I was mesmerized by it, taking it out of the case and putting it back in the case—over and over and over. There was something about the texture of leather and metal together that has stayed with me throughout my life. Within days, I was convinced that, thanks to this gadget, I had found evidence of radioactive material in the house. The meter's moving needle did not lie. Days later, the light meter's function as a detector had been converted into a radio. I swear I communicated with aliens. Then, one day, the meter's needle stopped moving, and I moved on. Other children might not have.

The same experience in the hands of a child driven by curiosity for moving parts would have ended differently. The light meter would have been disassembled by a fascinated youngster who would grow up to become, most probably, an engineer, surgeon, mechanic, burglar—who knows?

Once children get beyond the early stages of simple, tactile discovery, their connection to things is driven by their imagination. What is more intriguing are the choices children make when it comes to props and items. For them, physical reality is not limiting. They are doorways through which young minds enter into a world of unforeseen possibilities.

It is an interesting fact that the celebrated British thespian and film actor, Laurence Olivier (Hamlet, Henry V, Richard III, Pride and Prejudice, Wuthering Heights, Boys From Brazil, Marathon Man, Sleuth), could not begin to develop a character until he had a prop in his hand. What kinds of props did you use as a child? Do you still use props?

Make a list of things you reach for when you are thinking about important issues or when you are searching for ideas. Do you walk around the house and touch plants? Perhaps you grab a small figurine or object to help you focus. Using props in creative situations can be quite entertaining, especially when the actual function of the object is redefined for imaginary purposes.

WERE YOU ALONE OR WERE OTHERS INVOLVED?

Most of the time as a child, I lived in a world of my own. My games of pretending, especially at our summer cottage, were epics of exploration involving a cast of thousands in my head. During the school year, I did play with others and often took a leadership role. But I enjoyed sharing ideas and listening to the ideas of others. Who I am today is a direct reflection of those experiences. My work as a Writer-Producer-Director puts me in situations where I lead and direct, but also work collaboratively with creative teams and clients. What about you?

When you played games of pretend, which ones did you indulge in on your own and which ones did you find yourself engaged with others, whether in pairs or in a group? How does your creative interaction manifest itself today? When operating creatively, wherever you feel most comfortable usually reflects your pretending experience as a child.

The challenge is to move outside of your comfort zone to discover new creative experiences and relationships. This fresh approach will stimulate your creativity, even if it takes a little time to become comfortable.

WHAT ROLE (INCLUDING YOU) DID EVERYONE PLAY?

Leader, follower, subordinate, advisor, teacher, cheerleader, victim, champion, problem solver, caregiver, foil, tyrant, collaborator—what roles did you and others assume in your pretending games? Your role choices were probably shaped through family and school experiences and even the media you consumed.

You may have been someone who preferred to have a role assigned to you. Perhaps you designated roles to others. When you pursue a creative agenda today as an adult, how does your role and the roles of the people around you become defined? The role map that emerges from your analysis will reveal something about the way you engage in creative relationships. Note how the different roles you assume adjust to suit the type of creative agenda being pursued. For myself, some agendas are better served through my own, individual process.

Other agendas will motivate me to seek out my colleagues or friends, inviting collaboration.

Even more interesting is how a creative process is either enhanced or stifled within a more serious, committed relationship with a significant other. Hopefully, the art and science within these pages will help you realize how you can become acquainted with the creativity of others, allowing you to make a better connection with them.

When you recognize role choices others make in a creative process, it will enable you to adjust your participation without compromising your own creativity. Often, I become aware of individuals who are enthusiastically leading the pack without really taking the time to bring everyone equally into the loop. It's not that they are always domineering; simply, they are like an enthusiastic child with a passion for ideas and creativity.

I adjust my interaction with these types of people by acknowledging their ideas and gently steering things such that everyone gets a chance to provide input. Usually, the squeakiest wheel will settle down and blend into a more collaborative process. Enthusiasm is a wonderful thing. In most groups, it can be expected that at least one person will get into the mode I describe as *"Shoot—Ready—Aim."* If you need to remind yourself to be patient, think of a child you know who blurts out the first thing that comes to mind following the question, *"What shall we do to have fun?"*

Sometimes, even I find myself opening a creative flood gate with passion. There's nothing wrong with intensity as long as it doesn't shut down the other kids in the room. Take the time to sincerely pat these excited thinkers on the back, acknowledge their enthusiasm, and then invite the rest of the group to jump into the creative pool.

CHAPTER 7.

A FEW CREATIVE TRUTHS: VOLUME 2

1. How many things have you spent your lottery winnings on? Did you ever imagine saving any of it? Who did you share it with? What was the first thing you spent some of your winnings on? What did all of this creative thinking tell you—about you?

2. Speculation is one of the purest forms of intellectual creativity.

3. Diagrams on a napkin are proof of the ability to be creatively abstract. Unfortunately, we tend to throw napkins away. Bill Comrie, founder of the Brick, (one of North America's largest furniture chains), redesigned the structure of his stores based on a napkin drawing generated over lunch with his executive colleague, Kim Yost. He also came up with the very first Midnight Madness sale while as a young man on a date at a late-night, drive-in movie.

The promotion reinvented the way retailers think about promotions.

4. We create barriers, which, by implication, means we create problems and challenges worth solving.

5. At the moment you said, *"I give up!"* what happened next? The act of *giving up,* in many cases, is the first step to overcoming a barrier and opening the door to a creative solution to a problem or challenge. In order to experience the fullness of our own creativity, we need to be emotionally and intellectually free. It's not so much about *giving up* as it is about *moving on.* A dead end is a sign to turn around and keep going.

6. You can learn a lot about people by analyzing what they throw away in the garbage or the ideas they abandon. An airline once studied the content of post-flight garbage to determine what people didn't like to eat and modified the menu eliminating the meals passengers didn't enjoy. They saved millions of dollars and tons of waste.

7. If you want to generate ideas on how to succeed, make a list of all the things you need to do to fail;

then flip the list over (making the last thing first) and do the opposite.

8. If you want a creative think tank meeting to fail, start the process by asking for *good* ideas. Let me be blunt: *every* idea is inherently good, but, by branding the process with expectations, others will recoil into silence for fear that any idea they have is *not* good. Asking for *good* ideas is, at once, judgemental and a barrier to creative thinking. Rather, tell everyone that their ideas are important and the process will be fun. It will be an amazing, creative experience. Consider holding the meeting in a non-traditional environment.

9. Ask a child a simple question about solving a simple problem they can understand. You will learn something from the ideas they generate.

10. You don't buy a drill. You buy the hole it makes.

PART 3.

CHAPTER 8.

THE MATRIX OF INHERENT VALUES

---

*Advertisements must take into account not only the inherent
qualities and attributes of the products they are trying to sell,
but also in the way in which they can make those properties
mean something to us.*

—Judith Williamson

INTRODUCTION

Professor Judith Williamson is (at this writing) Professor
of Cultural History at the School of Communication and
Design at the University for the Creative Arts (UCA) in
the United Kingdom. In her book, "Decoding
Advertisements," she writes about the political and social
analysis of contemporary visual culture. Central to her
observations is that advertising imagery helps to define
the *"equation of people with things."*

In a book entitled "Advertising and Cultural Politics in
Global Times," Pamela Odih, a freelance journalist and
lecturer, refers to Williamson and further explained her
thinking by noting that *"advertisements have to translate
the 'inherent qualities and attributes of the products they sell'*

into statements that reflect human values and echo human relationships."

From my experience, the generation of ideas begins with the search to define these "inherent qualities." Regardless of what the ideas are applied to, which includes everything from advertising and love notes to problem solving strategies and inventions of any kind, inherent values trigger ideas. Anyone can find those triggers with the right coaching. Once we have a fundamental understanding of how creativity operates using inherent values, we can begin to bend the rules.

My father, an accomplished architect, believed that, in order to break the rules, you have to understand them. His process was to assess the land in order to envision the building. Pursuant to his thinking, without examining the environment within which we exercise creativity, we cannot innovate.

That is why the concept of "thinking outside the box" is the equivalent of designing a skyscraper without fully understanding the land it sits on. The same thing applies to ideation. If we are to find the ideas that lead to innovation, we have to understand what we know and how we think about the landscape of thought before we can generate solutions. That landscape includes beliefs, values, and meanings, which are already in place. They cannot be ignored.

Rewind. If there is anything "outside the box" and beyond what we know, it is the chaos of ignorance. We can, however, expand the box and stretch it. The edge of the box represents the boundary between our knowledge and our ignorance. Within the ideas on the edge are the innovative solutions, which advance our goals and transform our thinking. Beyond the edges is the vastness of our own ignorance.

Years before I discovered the term "inherent qualities" in marketing communications textbooks, I described my process of generating ideas as being a process based on "inherent *values*." For a period of time, I viewed the two terms, "quality" and "value," to essentially mean the same thing. I was wrong by definition and not alone when it came to missing the differentiation between the two terms. It is not unusual for people to use both terms interchangeably, but the distinction between the two is worth examining, especially if we are to appreciate how they actually work together.

"Function-Result" is an example of an Inherent Value (IVL) I use to trigger ideas. I suppose I could have simply called it an idea trigger, but when I examined the relationship between a drill, a hole, and a person, I asked myself, what ties them together? What makes the relationship work? The fact that the function of a tool is to make a workable result is an Inherent Value to the person using the tool.

So, "Function-Result" is the inherent value that gives meaning to the relationship a user has with any functional product or service. The dictionary is more specific, defining "value" this way: *"Value is that quality of anything which renders it desirable or useful."* Marketers often refer to quality and value as two distinct attributes. Their differences need to be highlighted to enable companies to produce better and improved products that have both quality and value.

Back to the dictionary. By definition, quality is an "attribute" and "value" is not. Value, as implied earlier, is defined as "desirability." It is also defined as a "precise meaning" or "significance." In summary, where quality is about attributes (like integrity, for example), value is about meaning (I value integrity because it helps me feel confident about the other person in the relationship). Still, I felt something was missing in my understanding of the difference between quality and value.

So, I examined the deeper, *emotional* connection that triggers a concept of value a consumer feels for any product or service—or idea for that matter. For example, in today's busy world, time is a commodity in short supply. Consider a product or service that saves people time. Safe to say, anything that saves time is appealing. Defining the benefit this way is accurate, but superficial. How does saving time *feel?* For me, it is a relief. Saving time frees me from worry, pressure and stress. That feeling of relief triggers the value I feel for something. How does this apply to the generation of ideas?

An idea on its own is like a drill still in the box. Until we use it, until we give it meaning, an idea is just an idea, a concept of something. Ideas are derivatives of a creative process. We give them value only when we act on them.

In Chapter 2, I explained a few things about the "Unique Selling Proposition" (USP), sometimes applied as a slogan. It is also important to understand that "USPs" and "inherent values" are connected, but *not* the same thing. Simply put, the USP is a singular expression (usually a brand in the advertising world) based on inherent values.

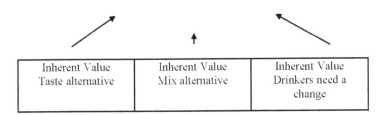

Unique Selling Proposition
"7UP, the Uncola"

Inherent Value Taste alternative	Inherent Value Mix alternative	Inherent Value Drinkers need a change

There are many types of Inherent Values (IVL), which can be categorized according to several contexts. These contexts include relationships and function. When advertising professionals are able to define the most relevant Inherent Values, they are then able to generate the creative thinking that leads to a USP/slogan or a campaign theme. Here are a few more examples of USPs specific to brand marketers, following which I will focus on Inherent Values.

- **FedEx:**
  "When your package absolutely, positively, has to get there overnight."

- **Coca-Cola:**
  "It's the real thing."

- **7UP:**
  "The Uncola."

- **DeBeers:**
  "Diamonds are forever . . ."

- **BMW:**
  "The ultimate driving machine."

- **M&Ms:**
  "The milk chocolate melts in your mouth, not in your hand."

- **Nike:**
  "Just Do It."

How do advertising professionals find the ideas that lead to these USPs or slogans? They will tell you that they first conducted consumer research to uncover and understand, as Williamson and Odih have explained, the intrinsic values associated with both the product and the consumer.

The creative thinkers for the agency who worked with Nike during the *"Just do it!"* campaign focused on the relationship people have with exercise and a healthy lifestyle. Their challenge was to come up with something that went beyond the traditional approaches agencies had been using with manufacturers and marketers of sporting equipment and clothing. The traditional approach was to focus on the attributes and benefits of the product. The problem was, many other brands in that category, such as Adidas and Reebok, were doing the same thing. Nike wanted to differentiate their brand, but had to find a new way of doing so. They started by researching the attitudes and perceptions their consumers had about Nike products.

What the consumer research helped them realize was that the focus was not just about buying shoes, sporting equipment or workout clothes. Rather, it was about their perceptions and attitudes toward a healthy and active lifestyle—and *feeling good* about it. These were critical values Nike considered. The values connected to the consumer's *feelings* about health and lifestyle were as significant as the values connected to the *function* of the product.

More interestingly, these values also applied to people who were *not* active. Less active people liked to wear Nike shoes and fashions because it gave them a sense of being active. In many cases, it was simply cool to wear Nike; it made them feel good even if they weren't particularly active.

It's a story about the relationship between two Inherent Values: a) the product's function and style, and b) people's desire to feel better about themselves and, in many cases, more appealing to others. It is human nature to want to be accepted, cared and loved by others. Nike dug a little deeper into this.

Deep down, people think about being active and healthy whether they actually experience that reality or not. Sometimes, we buy things thinking that we're going to follow-through. For example, we buy weight-loss products and never take the lids off the jars. We buy exercise equipment and never or rarely use it. We stock our bathrooms with vitamins and supplements that never find their way into our diet.

So Nike connected the dots and decided that the most effective way to make their brand appealing to both the active segment and inactive segment of the population was to challenge everyone to *"Just do it!"* And consumers responded by the millions and billions, buying shoes, clothes, sunglasses, rackets, clubs, balls, birds and head bands.

Nike's USP, *"Just do it!"* challenged the consumer it was targeting to get off their butts and get active, but it was a message targeting both people who would start jogging down the road as well as those who would never act on it, but would feel good anyway just thinking about it—while wearing Nike product, of course. Certainly, Nike would benefit more from those who accepted the call-to-action. The further we delve into the context of something we need an idea for and uncover the values, the more we provide ourselves with triggers for ideas. So, let's—just do it.

CATEGORIES & CLUSTERS

All matter originates and exists only by virtue of a force. We must assume behind this force the existence of a conscious and intelligent Mind. This Mind is the matrix of all matter.
—Max Planck

Max Karl Ernst Ludwig Planck, a German theoretical physicist, is the brain behind quantum theory for which he earned the Nobel Prize in Physics in 1918. A matrix is actually something we operate, mathematically.

For example, you can *"multiply a row vector by a column vector using a matrix."* Hunh? This function is drawn from Linear Algebra, the branch of mathematics concerning vector spaces and *computer* science, *computer* animation, and the social sciences.

On the other hand, there is the movie, "The Matrix." It

is biological, mathematical and digital in its conception. Ideation, too, needs a matrix within which various values operate: inherent values, contexts, points of view, attitudes, influences and ideas. Instead of employing numbers, the ideation matrix relies on language, including words, symbols and images. These elements influence and trigger our thinking and our ideas. To adapt Mr. Planck's point of view, the mind is the matrix of all creativity.

There are nine drivers of inspiration for ideas which I have defined over the years; nine Inherent Values (IVL) that stimulate different parts of your creative thought process and imagination. They invoke different images, experiences, and various emotional and intellectual contexts and responses. These Inherent Values are not exclusive, although you can choose to work exclusively with one IVL. They can also be combined. Inherent Values can also be found within other IVLs.

The categories of Inherent Values (IVLs or idea triggers) are termed as follows:

- Function-Result
- Cause-Effect
- Problem-Solution
- By Implication
- Negative Space Thinking
- The Other Alternative
- Proximity Influence
- Attitude-Altitude

- Shitz & Giggles

You can start an idea generating process with any IVL, and you can use several IVLs along the way. For example, if you are looking for ideas to address a problem, you would start your search for ideas using the Problem-Solution IVL. You might then shift gears and employ the Cause-Effect IVL because problems have causes. In all things, there are implications, which may be examined using the By Implication IVL. It will all add up to Actionable Ideas, which inspire solutions to the problem.

The IVL Hierarchy compartmentalizes the nine IVLs into three clusters, which are based on similarities. Within each cluster, some IVLs share stronger similarities, much like siblings, but they are still individually distinct. The fact that IVLs can function independently or together allows you to narrow or broaden your focus as you wish. It also ensures that the most varied points of view within a group will be enabled and engaged. Inherent Values are grouped together into three clusters according to their functions.

- Root Cluster
- Intuitive Cluster
- Associative Cluster

The **Root Cluster**, which includes the three IVLs, **Function-Result**, **Cause-Effect** and **Problem-Solution**, is a basic way to start the idea generation process. A leads to B. When something happens, something else happens.

Most ideation objectives are usually connected to a thing, product, service, process, situation—something very tangible or easily defined, whether its form is physical or defined by a series of steps or actions. If you are pursuing ideas relating to a product or service, the Function-Result IVL is highly relevant. The Idea String is sparked quickly.

Cause and effect characterizes what happens owing to actions, changes or shifts invoked by behaviors, economics, politics, new technologies, disasters—anything where a change in conditions results in a change in situations or circumstances.

For example, consistently higher prices on gasoline will lead to a rise in the sales of hybrids and electric vehicles. More electric vehicles on the road will lead to a demand for more charging stations—and so on. The Cause-Effect IVL can generate a remarkable Idea String, because it will germinate several branches along the way.

The Problem-Solution IVL has a strong connection to the Cause-Effect IVL, simply because problems have causes. When we analyze a problem, it requires us to find the causes, understand the effects, and evaluate the behaviors or processes being affected. The solution is either a resolution of something negative or the realization of something positive, such as an opportunity.

These three root IVLs share a *this-then-that* similarity. It can also be stated as, "*If this, then what?*" This cluster is the most rooted environment within which to generate an Idea String and, ultimately, Actionable Ideas with highly tangible specifications.

The **Intuitive Cluster**, which includes the next three IVLs, **By Implication**, **Negative Space Thinking** and **The Other Alternative**, is the portal to intuitive thinking;

seeing the unseen, actively listening to what we have only been hearing with distraction and paying more attention to the hunches or random thoughts we experience when we are pursuing ideas. Each of these IVLs are intuitive gateways. When we consider such things as a theme for an event, a headline for a newsletter, poster or advertisement, a concept for a story (article, book, screenplay, poem, speech), or a way to improve a personal or professional relationship, we reach into our intuition and our imagination to find the ideas that will give life to the intangible.

Certainly, if we are focused on improving a relationship, it might start with a search for ideas using the root IVLs, Problem-Solution and Cause—Effect. But, when emotions are involved, it challenges us to dig a little deeper into the intuitive landscape. This is where these intuitive IVLs perform effectively.

The By Implication IVL can either work quickly or be elusive, even mysterious. Most implications sit naked on the surface. To find the ones lurking deeper requires a degree of trust in your instincts.

The implications of some of the most devastating terrorist acts we have witnessed in our time, such as 9/11 and the Boston Marathon, have led to longer processing times through security and more flights missed. The implications are characterized by the higher stress levels experienced among travelers and airport staff. Dig a little deeper and we can see implications for services that reduce the stress time, such as online check-in, valet parking service, and premium airport waiting lounges. Airports evaluated these issues and understood the implications. Subsequently, the investment pool in specialized customer travel services has seen a substantial injection.

Moving on. The Negative Space Thinking IVL (NST) works well in situations involving hidden agendas within personal and professional relationships, political manoeuvring (especially during elections), and corporate or brand manoeuvring (especially in highly competitive industries).

As a creative tool, NST is tailor made for writers, especially for those who write stories, books or screenplays in the crime, mystery and psychological thriller genres. However, it can be applied in almost every genre. There is a plethora of examples: movies such as Christopher Nolan's "Memento" and books such as Dan Brown's "Da Vinci Code." All a writer needs to do is analyze the top fifty novels and movies known for their twists and learn how Negative Space Thinking works.

NST also serves strategic development agendas relating to innovations in product or service delivery development, research in any field or industry, or situations involving political and legal manoeuvring as mentioned earlier. Lawyers will enjoy a dose of NST in their strategic case preparations. Usually, the idea objective is clear, but the path to get there is complex.

Negative Space Thinking challenges us to listen more closely, to hear the things not spoken, and to see things we either have not noticed or to see them again for the first time with a new set of eyes. It compels us to engage our intuition, which usually senses issues, which have not been revealed. NST creates *"Ah ha!"* moments. The moment someone says, *"I feel we're missing something,"* or, *"We've tried everything; why isn't it working?,"* there is an opportunity to focus the conversation on speculation and analysis. The elusive implications are often hidden in plain sight. Strategic concepts such as, *"The best defence is a good offence,"* and *"The strongest position in negotiation is silence,"* are examples of ideas derived through the application of NST.

Side bar. According to research, there are enough resources in the world to feed every man, woman and child on the planet. Yet, close to 800 million people in the world do not have enough to eat. Those are the people in negative space. According to the World Food Programme, if **women** farmers had the same access to resources as men, the number of hungry in the world could be **reduced by up to 150 million**. That's one solution hidden in plain sight.

The last IVL in this cluster, The Other Alternative, shares some similarities with NST, but the focus is on alternatives. One doesn't have to go very far to generate a short list of alternatives relating to any main issue or objective. The Other Alternative is the less obvious one, often hidden inside other alternatives or within implications.

All the IVLs in this cluster are driven by intuition. When you are generating ideas and feel a hunch or a thought occur to you, which may not, at first, seem relevant to the objective you are focused on, stop and consider it. Write it down. Keep looking at it. See it from a different point of view by sharing it with someone else, even if they are not directly involved with your project or objective. An Actionable Idea will emerge.

The third cluster, the **Associative Cluster**, includes the last three IVLs, **Proximity Influence**, **Attitude-Altitude** and **Shitz & Giggles.** They are the portal to associations that are either implied or created. These associations, direct or indirect, trigger ideas involving language, images, behaviors and characters.

The Proximity Influence IVL is most effective when we create associations by design. The best springboard to launch an Idea String using Proximity Influence is to define the elements to be associated based on brand. Brands can be anything related to identity: a company or organization brand, product brand, philosophy, ideology, culture, community—even an individual brand (who you are). In the context of idea generation, associations are creative equations between brands. The key is to assess the points of view (POV) relating to the association being made. There are POVs on both sides of the association and it is critical to understand how these POVs affect it.

The application of associations leverages credibility, integrity and buy-in. For example, when it is not enough to make direct, quality statements, evidence of value is established using credible spokespeople to enhance and sell the message or idea. Politicians need celebrity endorsements because politicians are often perceived through POVs infected with a lack of trust.

On another level, a teacher selling an idea to a department head may need the backing of parents to achieve the objective. We can also identify associations through Proximity Influence between such things as events and behaviors. Valentine's Day associates with romance. Father's Day and Mother's Day associate with respect, acknowledgement and caring.

Every association has any or all of these elements: language, images, symbols, behaviors and characters. It's like an all-you-can-eat smorgasbord of creativity. You can easily mix and match, selecting the most relevant associations to trigger the most meaningful ideas. When we are trying to create a stronger position through association, the question we should be asking ourselves is, *"If I want to get the attention or buy-in to what I am proposing or offering, what or who do I need to connect to in order to leverage my position?"*

Speaking of position. No matter what your walk or talk is, I encourage you to read the marketing classic, *"Positioning, the Battle for Your Mind,"* by Al Ries and Jack Trout. The term, 'positioning,' was coined by Jack Trout in 1969. Ries and Trout were also the minds behind *"Bottom Up Marketing,"* which introduces the notion that an entire marketing plan can be developed from a tactic, rather than the other way around. Dominoes Pizza used their strategy by defining the tactic first (pizza in 30 minutes) and then built their entire marketing plan based on this tactic. It was brilliant. It influenced the marketing industry's thinking at a foundational level. The industry quickly adopted it. Back to POVs.

Earlier, I mentioned how individual POVs and attitudes influence and affect the idea quest. When the Attitude-Altitude IVL is applied, it gives us a license to leverage and amplify those POVs and attitudes. We can also force a POV or attitude into the mix to see what happens. If the objective is to create demand for something through promotions and advertising, we need to get inside the POVs and attitudes of the consumers being targeted.

If a politician wants to win an election, the strategy team will want to get inside the minds of the voters. If a woman wants to understand a man, she can try to think like a man. Sound familiar? (*Try this experiment at your next meeting. Ask all the women to think and respond from a man's POV and vice versa. Enjoy.*)

Perhaps the most interesting things to be discovered

through the process of shifting or adopting a different attitude are the various associations people will make, especially when they step outside their own characters and create new ones. Actors will tell you how the characters they portray affect their own, personal perceptions, some of which remain with them for the rest of their lives. There's a little bit of the actor in all of us. Use it. You're never too old to engage in the game of pretending.

Sometimes, all we need to trigger ideas is a random experience. Word association exercises, expressions of random thoughts, the Rorschach test (the inkblot test)—the first thing that comes to your mind—trigger associations spontaneously. The Shitz & Giggles IVL reduces the need to rationalize ideas, other than to make the connection to the objective once the Actionable Ideas are defined. When time is of the essence, this IVL gets things going quickly. It also serves as an add-on to a think tank process that has already invested time applying a different IVL.

Random, spontaneous idea generation without limitations (maybe a theme, loose or otherwise) is how children operate creatively. By not limiting the associations we make between terms or concepts, we generate quick lists and spur the process on. Once a list is generated and Actionable Ideas are established, it is possible to work backwards through the objective and find other associations that may have been missed.

The Shitz & Giggles IVL is a 2-way, creative side-street. It is also a one-size-fits-all IVL. The creative exercises associated with it are not intimidating and inhibited participants feel comfortable to engage more readily and openly. If the people in your group are conservative, lack confidence, or are simply not highly motivated to get fully involved, this would be the place to start the idea quest. To trigger ideas, you need to trigger the people.

The associations harvested using the IVLs in the Associative Cluster, in and of themselves, are Actionable Ideas. The associated implications are also ideas and will inspire other Actionable Ideas. Associative IVLs generate a very rich Idea String quickly, because most associations are easy to identify. Individuals of all types, especially in groups, are more eager to engage creatively, thanks to the fluid nature of these IVLs.

There is one caveat affecting everything in this book. Try not to view the concepts and steps as a recipe. Think of it more as an intuitive menu, which easily adapts to your creative process, whether it is linear, step-by-step progression, or non-linear, wherein there are many starting points allowing for expansion in many directions. Most importantly, allow yourself the opportunity to experiment.

There is no right or wrong in creativity. Sometimes, the first idea you generate is the road sign pointing toward your creative destination. Small ideas will accumulate, merge and even purge other ideas. The result is cumulative, leading to Actionable Ideas. It requires a little faith and perseverance and you are free to reach out at any time to a different Inherent Value that you have not exploited and let the creative winds carry you where they may.

We can also think of IVLs as idea triggers. IVLs are defined by the relationships we have with values and influenced by our points of view, POVs. These relationships occur between people and other people, people and material things or products and services, people and situations, people and actions or ways of operating, and people and philosophies, concepts, morals, desires, and emotions. These relationships give meaning to Inherent Values, which, in turn, spark ideas.

There are qualities within qualities, values within values, ideas within ideas. There is always something inherent within something inherent—a universe of creativity expanding both ways.

CONTEXT, IDEA STRINGS & ACTIONABLE IDEAS

The value of your idea is in its context.
—Rick van der Wal

In an article about ideation posted on Crinid.com, a wonderful website devoted to" *refreshing insights in the process of creating great ideas,"* Rick van der Wal underscores the importance of what happens *before* we apply our ideas. *"Context is a way to determine perspective and perception and follow it through to the benefits of implementation."* Creative think tanks do not always back track enough before launching into the process of generating ideas.

The methodology follows three steps: **The Context**, **Idea Strings** and **Actionable Ideas**.

The Context establishes the situation requiring the idea and the Inherent Value that is most appropriate to start working with. It may begin with an examination of causes to a problem and the history of events leading to a current situation. It may be researched through data such as analytics revealing trends, sequences, cycles, attitudes, and behaviors.

The context also establishes the POVs that are most relevant, especially those of the target market, group, community, or individuals. We can also target a behavior or a common benefit (referred to in marketing as "benefit segmentation") rather than simply defining the type of people we want to connect to based on demographics (quantifiable statistics such as household income).

After the Context is established, the **Idea String** is generated, a road map of ideas leading to Actionable Ideas and is represented by (and not limited to) any of the following:

- Language, including words, phrases, descriptive or narrative sentences, explanations, definitions, quotes, literary examples, colloquialisms, puns, original expressions, slogans, strategic statements, hypothesis, theory, conjectures, assumptions

- Images, symbols, sound (NOTE: these may either be the raw creative elements or a description of same)

- Artistic, scientific, academic or technological specifications

- Animate and inanimate objects, organisms, anything with physical dimensions

An Idea String can be populated with many of the things identified in the aforementioned list. Anything goes, really. Any expression of an idea is simply that; it can be abstract, oblique, specific, technical, artistic, quirky, complex, simple, fun, provocative, inspiring, bewildering, meaningful—but—never meaningless. The more ideas we record, the greater the number of Actionable Ideas we will generate.

An idea in the string can be expressed as speculation. *"The increasing frequency with which gas stations run out of fuel is an indication that oil prices may continue to rise."* That statement might be called a few things: an extrapolation, guess, fact, speculation, or an irrelevant comment. Regardless, it's an idea that leads to an Actionable Idea.

Other ideas in the string may ultimately become the Actionable Idea. For example, if you were generating ideas for a slogan, the idea would be expressed as a series of slogan concepts or value statements that can lead to a slogan concept.

An Idea String can be as short or as long as you make it. Exploration and experimentation will help you discover aspects of your own style or approach to ideation. When we add new information to this creative process, we continue to push the edge of the box outward.

Actionable Ideas are found within the Idea String and there may be more than one Actionable Idea generated. These are the ideas that define the solution. An Actionable Idea will be the slogan, theme or headline you were looking for (as I just covered). It will be the articulation of your next innovative step. It will be one of the answers to your problem. The Actionable Idea, as a tangible, creative result, inspires, promotes and gives form to the actions you want to take to realize the stated objective.

POINTS OF VIEW (POV) & ATTITUDES

If that's all there is my friends, then let's keep dancing.
—Lyric by Peggy Lee

If that's all there is, then, shoot me. It irks me when I hear, *"Well, that's the way it is."* If that's the way it is, I wouldn't have written this book. Unless we're talking about the Rockies, mosquitoes or compost, then, *the way it is,* is a derivative of choices made. We create the way it is. That's my point of view. What's yours?

No matter which IVL we use to help us find ideas, the idea quest is influenced and shaped by points of view (POVs), attitudes and behaviors. Our experience of life challenges us to cope, motivates us to achieve, scares us into protecting ourselves and others, and leads us in and out of relationships.

We feel, believe, judge, evaluate, accept, reject, debate, influence and act on what we know from our POV, which, in turn, shapes our attitudes. It is what *self* is all about. Self is self-ish. Many have told me that they believe any kind of selfishness is a negative thing. My POV is that there are certain kinds of selfishness we need in order to survive.

I am selfish and not always self-centered. My experience of life happens from behind my eyes. My mind interprets life for me. Absolute reality is something none of us know and, if you think you do—well—that's your POV. There are over 7 billion interpretations of reality. Sometimes we connect our POVs to share life and create a collective reality for the time we are together. Someone once speculated about the possibility of exchanging minds for 10 seconds and figured the shock would kill us. Maybe it would be exhilarating. Who knows? Until such time as it may be possible, it is science fiction for now.

The Inherent Values I have defined are a selfish interpretation of the creative reality I know based on my experiences working in the creative communications world. Your POVs are real—to you. That's why, if that's just the way it is, then that's the choice being made. The question now is, *"How is it going to be?"*

The application of the nine IVLs will help you gain a greater understanding and appreciation for your own POVs as well as those of the people around you, be it family, friends or colleagues. POVs can change, shift and be altered by self choice and by external forces, generally by both at the same time. POVs are neither right nor wrong, except for those that are harmful and destructive. We may invalidate each other, disagree, come together—whatever we do, it is a function of individual POVs applied at the same time, either adversely or collaboratively.

When operating creatively within a group, individuals take one of four positions. They lead, collaborate, follow or do little or they do nothing at all. In the best case scenario, the group's attitude comes together generating creative momentum. In effect, there is a slight shift from a selfish point of view to a selfless point of view as the group coalesces.

When there is conflict, the group can become mired in the minutiae and forget the big picture. Whether the situation is positive or negative, broad or myopic, there is really only one POV you know absolutely. Yours. It influences your attitudes and behaviors and how you act in response to fears or desires. The more we understand our POVs, the better a group can operate effectively in generating Actionable Ideas.

In the next chapter, we will look at the application of IVLs in detail. It is the *how-to* section. Before you jump in, take a moment to assess your POVs around creativity. How do you now view your creativity? How do you view the creativity of others?

Ultimately, my quest is to stimulate your creative thinking. It might be more accurate to say that the intention with *"A Brilliant Idea Every 60 Seconds"* is to trigger the parts of your brain that actually do the stimulating. For some, the idea that the brain is thinking when the mind is not aware of it may be nonsense. As Dr. Seuss put it, *"I like nonsense; it wakes up the brain cells."*

THE INHERENT VALUE MATRIX

WHAT DO YOU NEED AN IDEA FOR?
Articulate the objective requiring ideation.
EG. Need to solve a problem. Need a theme. Need to change, modify or innovate.

CONTEXT
Establish the context: situations, attitudes, behaviors, trends, sequences, cycles target markets, groups, communities, individuals, segments based on benefit or impact; Describe the Points of View (POV) and attitudes affecting or associated with the context.

Root Cluster	Intuitive Cluster	Associative Cluster
Function – Result Inherent Value: leads to making, doing and creating, giving meaning and value to the process, which triggers ideas.	**By Implication** Inherent Value: invites a deeper & broader examination of anything on which we are focused creatively.	**Proximity Influence** Inherent Value: creates implications by design through influence & association, particularly with strong, recognizable brands.
Cause – Effect Inherent Value: actions and events generate consequences, positive & negative, which stimulate the motivation to act. Actions taken are either reactive or proactive.	**Negative Space Thinking** Inherent Value: takes us to beyond looking to seeing, beyond hearing to listening, & beyond thinking about feelings & ideas to feeling & being in the moment. Intuition flourishes through which we give meaning and generate ideas.	**Attitude – Altitude** Inherent Value: alters & shifts points of view, leading to a discovery of more attributes (qualities), and meanings (values), which trigger Actionable Ideas.
Problem – Solution Inherent Value: motivates an analytical examination of causes within which ideas are found leading to a solution.	**The Other Alternative** Inherent Value: enables us to look forward, backwards, sideways, up, down, in, out.	**Shitz & Giggles** Inherent Value: distracts us from preconceived notions; allows the process of idea generation to be organic

IDEA STRINGS
Lists can include:
Language, including words, phrases, descriptive or narrative sentences, explanations, definitions, quotes, literary examples, colloquialisms, puns, original expressions, slogans, strategic statements, hypothesis, theory, conjectures, assumptions;
Images, symbols, sound;
Artistic, scientific, academic or technological specifications;
Animate and inanimate objects, organisms, anything with physical dimensions

Actionable Ideas

PART 4.

CHAPTER 9.

INHERENT VALUES—THE HOW-TO

For each Inherent Value (IVL) in this chapter, you will be provided with an overview of how each one works. At the end of each subsection is a step by step description of the process including the Context, Idea String, Actionable Idea, followed by a simple example and a summary of the type of people and situations that can best benefit from its application. (*The fact is, just about anyone can benefit from any IVL's application.*)

FUNCTION-RESULT

The function of prayer is not to influence God,
but rather to change the nature of the one who prays.
—Soren Kierkegaard

Kierkegaard, the Danish philosopher, theologian, poet, social critic, and religious author, was described as the first existentialist philosopher. It was his contention that individuals—not society or religion—give meaning to life. He positioned existence *before* essence.

Looking at it using the Function—Result IVL, the drill functions to create the resulting hole, but it is the hole that gives meaning to the drill and, by implication, gives meaning to our intentions for its use. The drill exists. The hole is the essence. Put another way, when you buy a drill, what are you buying? A tool, of course. Actually, *you are buying a hole.* The drill-hole example exemplifies a direct connection between product and function, and function and result.

Connecting this within the creative context of this book, creativity is the drill (function); ideas are the holes (result). Our application of these ideas gives meaning to creativity. Too often, we muse and stew when we generate ideas, hoping we will just *come up* with an idea. It is as if we have a drill in our hands and hope the realization that it makes a hole will come to us. What if we know and trust from the beginning that an idea, like a hole, is inevitable? So rather than focusing on ideas, we focus on *defining the intrinsic values of any given function and what our relationship is to that function.*

When we search for ideas, it is not uncommon to think about concepts without attaching a real process to it. We search our minds for some illusive gem, but the only context we have is that we need an idea for something. It would be no different than searching for a destination and staring at a map without any roads or towns marked on it.

By defining the relationship through its qualities and values, in this case the function and the result, we begin to shape ideas almost immediately, putting destination marks on the creative road map. This relationship enables the user to create. You might ask, *"How does a home help someone create something?"* Don't forget, we create experiences through our homes: parties, celebrations, family life.

Usually, these actions lead to positive feelings, like a sense of accomplishment. *"I saved money." "I created something interesting and that makes me feel good about myself." "I learned something I didn't know before, which I can now apply to many other things that I like to do, need to do, or would like to try and that makes me happy and motivated."* The simple benefit of a *feeling of accomplishment* is very limited in its expression. When we take the time to listen to the thoughts people express as a result of feeling something (like accomplishment), we embrace a much deeper understanding of the perceived value from the POV of the person feeling the value.

In a sense, we can look at things through their eyes. This triggers ideas of how we can develop other products and services for them and how we communicate with them through advertising mediums and other communication channels, including emails, blogs and comments. Now we can actively get their attention instead of guessing at how we attract their interest.

Every product or service with a function has an intended result. How we connect to that relationship is enabled by our intentions. We drive a certain kind of vehicle because we need transportation. Our own personal transportation gives us freedom, not only to move around, but to discover new things and new adventures.

We also have lifestyle needs, which includes ego, implying a desire to be accepted. The vehicle we drive reflects on who we are. We want to be perceived a certain way. A Lamborghini says one thing. A Caravan says another. These are the kinds of aspects we need to understand before we begin to generate ideas. Why and how do people use a product or service and how do they feel about it? The answers are ideas.

When we examine all of the elements within the Function-Result IVL—the functional enablers, the tangible results, and the feelings or perceptions associated with those results—ideas and concepts emerge almost automatically.

Ergo: the Inherent Value of Function-Result is that it leads to (or enables) making, doing and creating, giving greater meaning and value to the process, which triggers ideas.

To set up a process of generating ideas using the Function-Result IVL, follow these steps.

Establish the Context.

- Describe the function of a product, service, relationship or process. What is it designed to do? How does it function? Is it simple or complex to use?

- List the results it produces. What does the product enable the user to do or experience?

- Are the effects of the results short-term or long-term? If the product or service is complex, it may require a longer timeframe to apply the Actionable Ideas. It might also be the function of a cycle and a degree of planned repetition might be required.

- How do users feel about the results created? How does it affect, improve or change their life? List the feelings and behaviors associated with the results achieved, the statements of which might look something like these: *"It frees up time providing relief from stress." "It provides peace and security." "It inspires and motivates users to be creative and adventurous." "It peaks curiosity." "It fuels innovation and builds confidence."*

Generate the Idea String.

- Examine the connections between various functional aspects revealed through the answers or lists generated through your examination.

- Pay close attention to the tone of the language. Examine the terms, phrases and expressions used to describe functions, attributes, values and meanings.

- List images and symbols associated with elements in the Idea String.

Example. Develop a creative concept for a demolition company involved in a golf tournament.

The Context. A demolition company is sponsoring a golf tournament. The objective is to make them as visible as possible.

The Idea String. List all of the functional issues relating to golf: the golf club, ball, golf cart, golf course, etc. Every sport has its own colourful lingo and is a fertile-rich seed-bed for ideas.

The game of golf is replete with colourful language including many terms, turns of phrase and expressions. List terms and turns of phrase associated with golf. List the language elements and expressions making note of anything that may have a connection to the context of demolition. *"On the screws." "Be the hole." "Ball must have said something to the hole." "In the hole." "Air mail." "You crushed it."*

The Actionable Idea. *"You crushed it."* connects thematically to the demolition company. The next step was to examine synonyms to the term "crush." This connected the idea to the term, "demolish." The concept, which was conceived and applied by my good friend, Dennis Gane, was to stamp promotional balls with the company's logo and the statement, *"Demolish me."* In fact, Dennis generated the idea first and then pitched it to the demolition company hoping to get their commitment to the tournament. It worked.

The Application. For people who market and sell products, which includes the people who write about it (such as ad writers, online copy writers, etc), the Function-Result IVL will provide ideas that will relate well to marketing or advertising.

It is particularly helpful for people developing SEO (Search Engine Optimization) strategies and who are searching for the strongest keywords and phrases. It provides insights to consumer thinking and how the SEO strategy might be developed or enhanced. Of course, Google Analytics is a go-to starting point and provides the most popular keywords and phrases at a glance. They become even more relevant when they are connected to trends in attitudes and behavior.

This IVL also assists anyone involved with the design and development of products. If you are in marketing or sales, this IVL serves several sides of the equation: product/service design, distribution, merchandising, advertising, promotion and retention.

It is also helpful for anyone engaged in the production

of instructional and marketing videos or publications focused on products and services.

So, how can Function-Result be applied to relationships and processes? Consider that a relationship creates a result, so it serves as a function. A marriage is the result of a relationship between two people who assume they won't get divorced. A process also serves a function. An assembly line is a functional process. One might refer to everything as a product. A divorce is a very valuable product to lawyers.

CAUSE-EFFECT

Cause and effect are two sides of one fact.
—Ralph Waldo Emerson

As previously stated, the Cause-Effect IVL is often linked to the Problem-Solution IVL. In the context of generating ideas, understanding cause and effect is a first step before diving into the search for a solution to a problem. An example. Single parents are challenged by time. At the end of a busy day, they still have to function as nurturers and care givers, which means they have to feed their children, chauffeur them to activities and do all of this while trying to find some down time for themselves. The commodity they are in need of most is time itself.

This was the issue companies like MacDonalds learned more and more about as they evolved. They recognized that *lack of time* was affecting millions of people in a world where the population of single parents was rising exponentially in the wake of rising divorce rates. How productive divorce is.

Eventually, the food retail industry introduced "ready-made" and "ready-to-go" meals in their deli sections because they realized that all families, not just single parent families, were affected by the time drought. It didn't stop there. The success of the internet can be attributed, in part, to the consumer's voracious desire for convenience.

Most retailers will tell you that consumers spend more time at home researching their purchases before stepping out of the house to go shopping. Lack of time is a powerful example of how a single cause and effect issue can change everything.

Think about cause and effect in your life. How has time affected you? The Cause-Effect IVL can help you, your team or your organization solve problems—and create opportunities. Life is influenced by outside forces and our own actions; some effects are obvious, some not.

When I studied Economics at university, I was profoundly influenced by the larger scale relationships and how events affected everything from politics to social behavior. For example, I am particularly interested in how the aging baby boomer demographic is becoming larger and larger statistically as a component of senior populations, particularly in North America, and how that exponential growth is impacting various sectors such as travel, employment, healthcare, real estate development and the manufacturing of commodities as well as niche products. Many manufacturers and marketers are targeting them specifically. It is the modern day Gold Rush or, more accurately, Old Rush.

Switching focus. The increasing incidents of disasters

caused by weather, earthquakes, terrorism and massive industry failures such as oil spills and nuclear disasters have motivated the World Bank to establish a significant fund dedicated to supporting vast relief efforts around the world, a fund that did not exist until 2006 when they established the Global Facility for *Disaster* Reduction and *Recovery.*

The internet, as a disruptive technology, is beginning to fuel significant concerns around privacy. It is also forcing core media such as television, radio and print to reassess their futures. The mega communication companies are downsizing rapidly. Many of my colleagues have lost their jobs.

However, there is an upside. Entrepreneurs are pitching their concepts and ideas through crowd funding websites rather than seeking loans from banks. The crowd-funded project base is putting thousands to work. Thanks to the internet, we are able to broaden our search for solutions and new ways of doing things, starting up ventures in home offices and exploring possibilities.

Indeed, phone mobility and applications are transforming the way we do everything from managing our day to day routines, finding our destinations, considering our shopping options, and deciding on entertainment. One day, there will even be an app for brilliant ideas.

Cause and effect generates consequences. This inspires ideas, sometimes out of desperation. The feelings associated with events invoked by cause and effect are often flavoured with confusion, angst and concern. On the flip side, we can feel optimistic and excited, especially when the effect ignites opportunity. For example, the demand for content and innovative programs for distribution on the web is through the roof. Disruptive technology inspired a myriad of opportunities for developers and producers.

Ergo: the Inherent Value of Cause-Effect is that actions and events generate consequences, both positive and negative, which stimulate the motivation to act. The actions taken are either reactive or proactive.

To set up a process of generating ideas using the Cause-Effect IVL, follow these steps.

Establish the Context.

- Describe the causes and effects associated with your situation. The causes may be expressed as conditions, circumstances or behaviors. Note what is known and not known. Describing something not known might look like this: *"We know we are losing clients. We don't know why we're losing clients."* One idea that springs forth is to survey clients and customers who have been lost to determine causes.

- Categorize causes and effects: natural, manipulated, by design, accidental or unknown. You might identify additional categories.

- Are the effects short-term or long-term? The Actionable Ideas may need to be applied within a certain cycle or timeframe. It may require a series of Actionable Ideas over a period of time in order to generate the intended results.

Generate the Idea String.

- Examine the connections between various causes and effects revealed through the answers or lists generated through your examination. Identify and list any trends or similarities within the causes and effects.

- How do they positively or negatively affect the situation? List the substantive changes including the feelings and behaviors associated with the effects and consequences incurred, which might include animosity, resentment, anxiety, frustration, curiosity, ambition, anticipation and control to name a few.

- Pay close attention to the tone of language. Examine the terms, phrases and expressions used to describe the circumstances surrounding the causes and the reaction to the effects.

- List images and symbols associated with elements in the Idea String.

Example. Develop a strategic understanding of the decline in enrolment in a Christian school.

The Context. An urban, Christian K to 9 school has been seeing a decline in enrolment for a few years. As there has not been a corresponding decline in population specifically affecting the number of families or children in the area, they believe they can reverse the trend.

The Idea String. Interview the people who answer the phone (receptionists and administrators) at the school. Ask them questions about the enquiries they receive, especially those concerning any students who have moved to other schools, as well enquiries relating to a potential new student. Also, interview families who have moved their children to other schools.

List the common questions and comments fielded through these enquiries. Draft a breakdown based on the kinds of people who have phoned in. Are they predominantly female or male, single parents, or relatives? How broad is the ethnic diversity? Also, where do they get their information about schools? What media do they consult to get community information: television, newspaper, radio, web? Who else do they talk to?

The research revealed that the majority of calls came from Mothers evenly split between two parent and single parent families. Among the top questions were those concerning bus transportation, the context of Christian education, and, surprisingly, the credentials of the school and its teachers.

The prevailing opinion was that there were several misconceptions and unknowns about the school. Word of mouth on the street was highly inaccurate. It was also becoming clear that ethnic diversity was increasing as new families moved into the area. Almost all of the callers said they engaged with all media to get their news and information about the community.

The Actionable Idea. The research produced the Actionable Ideas. The cause of the decline in enrolment was the result of an increasing number of ethnic families moving into the area as well as various trails of misinformation regarding the curriculum in the Christian school. At this point, the cause and effect scenario transformed into a clear problem-solution case study.

It was determined that a message was required to target Mothers frequently with information concerning the facts around the school's curriculum, credentials and bus transportation service. From the cost standpoint, radio offered the best options. The school purchased airtime, specifically a sponsorship of the weather report. Mothers listen to weather reports routinely so as to know how to dress their children.

The tone and manner of the message was designed as a one-to-one conversation between mothers, in which a soft-spoken woman imparted information on the school's curriculum, the scope of the bus service and the credentials of the school and its teachers. The commercials began with the radio mother saying, *"Let's talk about your child's education, mother to mother."* The effect of the radio campaign reversed the decline in enrolment.

The Application: The Cause-Effect IVL serves anyone pursuing a quest to understand issues and situations arising out of a shift or change in trends or circumstances. Usually, this implies a problem begging a solution. The example serves to underscore how the research itself populates the Idea String. Within the string are the Actionable Ideas. Whether you are searching for ideas to reverse a trend or improve a relationship, the Cause-Effect IVL will get you more than halfway to your solution.

If you are a team leader or project manager, this IVL is a valuable tool when dealing with issues and problems relating to your projects or assignments. It is also serves individuals focused on developing new products or chasing innovations for existing products or services.

PROBLEM-SOLUTION

Every problem has in it the seeds of its own solution.
If you don't have any problems, you don't get any seeds.
—Norman Vincent Peale

Problem-Solution is one of my favorite IVLs. It functions particularly well as a portal to ideas when a think tank is assembled by an organization or company to deal with critical issues.

What makes the Problem-Solution IVL truly effective is how it works in reverse. Most times, we are focused on finding solutions. If we embrace the meaning of the statement made by Mr. Peale, we can appreciate that the secret weapon within the Problem-Solution IVL is the opportunity to focus more on understanding the problem, in some cases, redefining it.

It may be a function of realizing that you (or your organization) are dealing with the wrong problem or the wrong context of the problem. In other words, the focus should be on how the problem is defined (the "seeds of its own solution"). There are different ways to look at a problem and find hidden intrinsic values you may have missed otherwise. Ultimately, when you nail the best definition or context to the problem, you usually nail the solution. At the very least, you find the best departure point to deal with it.

Back tracking briefly. The single parent scenario is a good example of how Cause-Effect links to Problem-Solution. Being a single parent led to a lack of time—cause and effect. A lack of time led to the creation of products and services focused on delivering convenience and quick access—solutions to the problem.

When we analyze causes, we can determine remedies (generating ideas) involving actions, devices or changes in behavior. It becomes an interesting loop: cause creates effect creates problem creates solution creates another effect (and sometimes, more problems). Between the problem and the solution is the space of time within which we generate ideas. So, it can be said that Cause-Effect exists within Problem-Solution.

When facing problems, we are best served by peeling away as many layers as we can to define the causes, which can be one or many: attitudes, beliefs, misinterpretation, false or misaligned expectations, lack of trust, hidden agendas, lack of knowledge or resources, defective parts or defective thinking, lack of preparation or training—it is a long list.

I remember reading through an education website, which divided problems into four main categories: easy, medium, ugly and hard. The fact is, each problem has its own category in addition to being easy, medium, ugly and hard. The good news is that there are solutions to problems 99.9 percent of the time. Usually, when we can't solve a problem, it is because, as individuals or as a group, we either choose not to pursue solutions, even if solutions have been defined, or we abandon solutions and give up.

Within the advertising and marketing world, Problem-Solution is referred to as an "activation method." You can recognize when the creative ad team based their approach on a Problem-Solution activation method. Typically, you will see or hear an ad that starts with something like the following.

- *"Suffering from back pain? Try this product."*
- *"If you're tired of pouring your money into your gas tank, maybe it's time to change the car your gas tank is in."*
- *"Not enough room in your closet? What if you could shrink everything?"*

Capella University, an online education resource, offers a comprehensive view of problem analysis. A visit to their site is worth the time to understand problem-solving techniques.
(www.capella.edu/interactivemedia/criticalThinking/3b_socratic.aspx)

In step two of their comprehensive process and within the analytical component, you are asked to separate symptoms from underlying causes. Identifying and understanding symptoms is how doctors work. Before there is any time applied to defining a cure (think of a cure as an idea), an examination of the symptoms is critical to the diagnosis. The symptoms help determine the triggers for illness or disease. The same, too, can be applied to the creative process, which leads to the generation of ideas. We can understand the symptoms of any situation to discover implications, which, in turn, trigger ideas.

The Problem-Solution IVL begs a dedicated commitment to analysis. Notwithstanding the emotions that can surface in a room where anxiety and the stifling smog of tension pervade, the generation of ideas to find solutions to problems requires an agreement between the participants to persevere. Problems and their causes, in and of themselves, are *not* barriers to success.

However, there is one common barrier: the unwillingness to work together to solve problems is the single, most limiting barrier. We resist and fight what we do not understand because it is easier. But, not all problems start as a negative experience.

"Success can be the first step to failure." This quote is not attributed to anyone, but, generally, the reverse of it, or something like it, is found in many quotes about success. This context of success leading to failure refers to individuals or companies who achieve success quickly and are not prepared for it. For example, a product becomes an overnight success, but the manufacturer cannot deliver enough units to meet the market demand in the short term, and the consumer decides not to wait and moves on.

Sometimes, success is overestimated, but it leads to unforgiving results. Kevin Costner's film, "Waterworld," initially attracted a lot of attention because he was at the height of his career. The movie was a bust at the box office.

Clairol thought it could expand their line of products into untraditional territory (for them) and easily gain share because of their existing brand recognition. In 1979, they fell flat with their Touch of Yogurt shampoo. I, too, would have a hard time wrapping my mind—and my hair—around the concept of washing with it. Clairol is not alone in committing this kind of *faux-pas;* I have my own success-leading-to-failure story.

Years ago, I developed a logline for a movie (a short one-line statement that defines the movie's story) and posted it on the internet—too soon. A couple of days later, I was contacted by Alliance Atlantis, a major film company at the time (later Alliance-Atlantis was sold to a consortium). The problem was that I did not have a script; just a logline, a concept of a story. The solution was to write the screenplay, which I finally did. Unfortunately, no one expressed a serious interest in it once it was posted. (Post mortem. Recently, I teamed up with a Canadian comedian who liked the story and encouraged me to rework it. *Never say never.*)

Whatever the problem is, it takes ideas to solve them. The best ideas are inherent in the cause or causes of the problem. It's a poetic conundrum—finding ideas to solve problems created by ideas.

Ergo: the Inherent Value of Problem-Solution is that it motivates an analytical examination of causes within which ideas are found leading to a solution. CAVEAT: cooperation and a dedicated commitment to sharing the process and discussion of analysis are contributing factors to success.

To set up a process of generating ideas using the Problem-Solution IVL, follow these steps.

Establish the Context.

- Describe the problem, listing known causes and effects as well as listing where causes are unknown, ensuring it is looked at from all POVs: the user, customer, client, team member and employee.

- Categorize the problem issues: procedures, knowledge, communication, physical layout, technology gaps.

- Are the issues intermittent, short term or long term?

Generate the Idea String.

- Identify any trends and similarities among the issues.

- List the feelings and behaviors associated with the various issues. (*Refer to the Cause Effect IVL as a cross reference.*)

- Examine the connections between various issues revealed through the answers or lists generated through your examination.

- List customer and employee comments. Pay close attention to the tone of language. Examine the terms, phrases and expressions used to describe the circumstances surrounding the problem.

- List any solutions that may have been expressed or suggested. Determine which suggestions have been followed up with and those that have been ignored or rejected. Examine why submissions were rejected. Sometimes, attitudes interfere with decisions and examining these attitudes can generate ideas for solutions.

Example. Develop a retail employee program to improve performance.

The Context. Staff absenteeism is increasing in frequency, leaving gaping holes on the floor. Staff turnover is increasing among sales people, but not supervisors and managers. Product returns are on the rise. There is a certain degree of animosity between staff and supervisors, evidenced by staff not always following through on directions given by supervisors. Not all supervisors and managers are disliked or ignored. Staff is also resistant to discussing internal issues.

The issues appear to be aggravated by a lack of communication among employees and the result of a lack of motivation, more so than a lack of available information. The performance in this store is specific to this store and does not appear to be manifesting as much in other stores within the chain.

The Idea String. Re-examine the training to determine the degree to which the causes are resident in the training material and the delivery of it. Is there enough emphasis being placed on knowledge retention? Was this considered in the design of the training program?

Find out what customers are thinking. Determine the trends within their opinions. What really ticks them off? What really turns their crank? Ask employees, too, what they believe customers are thinking. (This can be very revealing about the employees' attitudes and beliefs.)

Survey the employees to determine how they feel about their jobs, roles and functions. What works or doesn't work for them? How do they feel about the way they are trained, supervised and acknowledged?

Find out how they feel about responsibility and accountability. What do they enjoy at work and what motivates them? Most importantly, ask them what they think needs to be done to make them the best performing employee they can be. This is *not* about being the best performing employee in the store. Avoid creating a competitive, class system. Also, ask them to share ideas relating to any improvement in the store and how it operates.

The Actionable Ideas. Develop training media that helps employees understand the customer's POV. For example, create a series of training videos in which customers ask questions to employees. Have the customers speak directly to camera so that the employee, as the viewer, feels they are in the scene. Within the video scenes, feature the thought process of the customer as they listen to the employee. Avoid showing an employee in the video. Make sure the scenarios surprise the employees with the truth about how customers think. Educate them to expect that the unexpected is going on in the minds of consumers. Add humour where appropriate to retain their interest. These videos will help employees realize that their perceptions about customers are not always aligning completely with the reality.

Conduct an in-store survey of customers and make the survey highly visible to staff. Assume it will intimidate some employees, which will require a well-planned communication program to help employees feel comfortable with the objective of the survey; that it is not to point fingers, but rather to determine how training can be improved. Ask for employee input on the survey. This will begin to develop their buy-in to improved customer service and help them feel they are taking ownership of the process. Achieving employee buy-in is, perhaps, one of the most neglected areas in every business and sector.

Develop and implement programs of acknowledgement. Post biographical profiles of employees on a scheduled rotation in the employee common area. Celebrate the highlights of the employee's accomplishments outside of work and celebrate their achievements.

Develop and implement morale building programs. Create the *Coffee Mate* program. Have employees draw one name a month. At some point within the month at their own choosing, Employee A is required to bring Employee B their favorite beverage (excluding alcohol). The one caveat is that Employee B cannot be engaged with a customer or be in a closed meeting.

Offer a monthly reward (such as a monogrammed coffee cup or drinking glass) for the most creative presentation of a beverage to an employee. (*I established this program at the corporate head office of the retail chain where I worked. One presentation involved several employees dressed in 18th century costumes, presenting beverages on silver trays.*)

The Application. Whether you are a manager of a retail team or entrenched in a corporate structure, you may already know that the many issues faced with employees are not easily addressed through regimented communication plans or financial incentives. Employee research has often shown that money is not at the top of the list in terms of what employees need or want. *A desire for acknowledgement* shows up at the top of many lists. A dedicated commitment to humanize the work place will produce significant results in productivity and long-term commitment.

Employees eventually leave companies when they don't feel included in how the business operates or develops. The first sign of the problem is their performance. Their attitudes change because they do not feel cared about, valued or understood. If you are a manager, supervisor, executive, or a team leader, get to know the people you direct. Dig a little deeper to find the ideas that can become motivators and galvanize participation. Employees are always an excellent source of concepts and ideas.

BY IMPLICATION

Greater than scene is situation. Greater than situation is implication. Greater than all of these is a single, entire human being, who will never be confined in any frame.
—Eudora Welty

Pulitzer Prize winning American author, Eudora Welty, had an appreciation for inherent values and the power of implication. She wrote, *"Long before I wrote stories, I listened for stories. Listening for them is something more acute than listening to them. I suppose it's an early form of participation in what goes on. Listening children know stories are there. When their elders sit and begin, children are just waiting and hoping for one to come out, like a mouse from its hole."* That statement applies implicitly to the process of creativity and the generation of ideas. An idea can be like a mouse coming from within its hole.

Literally defined, implication is something *"suggested as naturally to be inferred or understood."* By applying inference, we read between the lines, leading to understandings that can reveal new ideas. Applied to the generation of ideas, it is always constructive and advances the creative process. If there is anything that prevents us from realizing this, it can be attributed to the limitations of our behavior and POVs, which get in the way of truly listening to what we hear and really see what we are looking at.

That is why, as Welty put it, children are hard wired to hear and see the stories and ideas, which allude most adults. The good news is that, as adults, we can reconnect to the nature of the creativity, which has always been within us since childhood, a nature buried under life's experiences; buried, but not silenced. Like sculptors, we need to remove the rock to reveal what has always been there. The value of identifying contexts and understandings using the By Implication IVL is that we focus more on establishing triggers for ideas rather than generating the ideas themselves.

As outlined previously, when analyzing a problem, we are better served creatively when we look deeper into the problem rather than navel gazing in the hopes that a solution will appear. Socrates, the Greek philosopher, was particularly fond of mining problems to solicit a deeper understanding of them rather than discussing solutions prematurely. Using a method now known as the Socratic Method (or Socratic dialogue or dialectic), he became famous for drawing out knowledge from his students by pursuing a series of questions and examining the implications of their answers. This critical thinking is still applied today, a legacy from a man who, ironically, never wrote any ideas down.

The By Implication IVL responds well to different styles of thinking and creativity. No matter how simplistic an implication may be, every idea put on the table is in play. *There is no such thing as a stupid idea.* Ideas, like IVLs, will also mix and match and transform, sometimes by design, and sometimes by accident, which I refer to as a creative accident. And I have had a few accidents.

When I was a young copywriter, I developed an ad campaign for a carpet cleaning company. The slogan I penned was, *"We love to clean!"* When I presented it to the owner, he leaned over his desk and said firmly, *"We do NOT love to clean. Are you kidding? No one in their right mind loves to clean. But we do take pride in what we do, more as a matter of survival, because we have to pay for mortgages and send our kids to school. So, we do not love to clean. We have to clean and clean well to make money. Thankfully, customers don't love to clean either, which keeps us in business."*

In that instant, my understanding of advertising and marketing was transformed. In terms of the carpet cleaning company campaign, there was never any implication that led to the idea I had developed. In fact, the idea was not derived out of a real understanding of the relationship between the service and the customer. One might say, I created a drill that makes squares. I had not stopped to consider the truth of the situation and the real relationship between cleaning and our domestic attitudes and behaviors. I had missed the real implications, something I would never do again.

There are implications in everything. They are either obvious or assumed, meaning we postulate without proof and, sometimes, we misinterpret a situation. It is a seesaw between logical and illogical reasoning, objectivity and subjectivity. Regardless, implications are the source of ideas and can even be ideas de facto.

The By Implication IVL functions with every other IVL described in this book. There are implications inherent in causes to problems, implications that arise from a change in attitude and so on.

When our intuition is engaged, we can see implications that are not so obvious. It is one of the most fertile breeding grounds for ideas and we are not limited by objectivity or subjectivity. Once we generate ideas, we also generate implications from those ideas. Ideas inspire ideas; they are all connected, even if the connection is oblique. Every implication, like every idea, has value. On the surface, it may not appear to be so, but I have seen obscure, simple, seemingly innocuous ideas and implications lead to amazing results.

Ergo: the Inherent Value of By Implication is that it invites a deeper and broader examination of anything on which we are focused creatively.

To set up a process of generating ideas using the By Implication IVL, follow these steps.

Establish the Context.

- Describe the situation breaking it down into as many aspects as possible: behaviors and attitudes, physical, functional, technical and emotional qualities and values, and the relationship users have toward the qualities and values.

- Note what is known and not known. Pay close attention to what is stated as *unknown,* because implications lurk within them. A quick example: the reason a product concept has not been advanced to market is because a) it has not yet occurred to anyone to do so; b) it has been tried and was not viable; c) it was not viable because—*the answer to this quite often leads to the Actionable Idea.*

- Progressively categorize conditions, circumstances, feelings, behaviors and assumptions according to a ranking starting with those aspects, qualities and values, which are clearly defined and self-contained, to those you feel have implications. You can also categorize aspects according to function, result, cause, effect, problem and solution.

- Separate tangible, physical aspects from philosophical, emotional and intellectual ones.

Generate the Idea String.

- Generate a list of implications for each aspect. Do not limit yourself. Implications may be direct or indirect. List both tangible and intangible implications.

- Examine the terms, phrases and expressions used to describe the implications to see how they may connect.

- List images and symbols associated with elements in the Idea String.

Example. The baby boomer population is aging. What are the implications?

The Context. This is a Canadian context although percentages closely resemble those in other countries. The desire for Active Adult Living is fueled by time, which is moving faster as the increasing numbers of the aging population grows rapidly. The number of seniors (age 65 and over) is over 5 million, the highest rate ever in Canada. The fastest-growing age group is 60–64 year-olds, at 29 per cent. Back in 1971, eight per cent of us were 65 and older. Within two decades, it's expected that 22.8 per cent of us will be 65 and older.

In 2012, about 8.1 million individuals, or 28% of Canadians aged 15 years and older, provided care to a family member or friend with a long-term health condition, disability or aging needs. The survey also found that care giving responsibilities most often fell to those aged 45 to 64, with 44% of caregivers in this age category.

The 2011 Census indicated that just over 7 per cent of seniors lived in a facility offering special care, such as a seniors' residence, long-term care facility, or chronic care hospital. For those aged 65 to 69 years, about 1 per cent lived in these types of residences. That number is increasing rapidly. The expansion of community-based elder care programs including in-home care is predicted to be an important factor both in containing costs, and in providing the kind of care that seniors and their families prefer.

Lastly, a whopping 85% of Canada's baby boomers plan to remain in their "home and native land" once they retire, according to a BMO Retirement Institute survey. Not surprisingly, given Canada's harsh winters, weather was the most cited factor motivating Boomers to relocate, cited by 57% of those surveyed. Financial reasons were next most cited at 54%, followed by proximity to family and friends (45%) and better access to health care and support services (35%).

At the end of the day, the aging population is not going anywhere and, for the next twenty years, close to half of them will be seeking a new living alternative within Canadian borders. Where will they go?

The Idea String. It is clear that there are three distinct audiences: a) the **aging boomer**; b) the 45 to 64 year old **care givers** and; c) the **individuals connected to baby boomers** who are affected by the decision making process around the living circumstances for aging seniors. The latter includes the children of baby boomers aged 19 to 39, who comprised 27% of the total population in 2011.

Another important statistic: 74 per cent of seniors (age 65 years and older) and 48 per cent of older adults (age 45 to 64 years) report having one or more of 11 chronic conditions. This increases the demand for care and places a burden on both health care and the family.

The implications include: a growing need for affordable, assisted living developments, an increasing burden on urban services as aging, rural, boomers flock to larger cities, and a demand for products and services catering to the aging population.

The Actionable Idea. Developments that provide a lifestyle suitable for seniors as well as assisted living opportunities are not a new concept. Christenson Developments in Alberta is at the forefront of this paradigm. But a new concept has emerged and is beginning to attract attention.

A group known as the Communities Development Society based in Calgary took a closer look at the implications affecting aging seniors in rural settings. The migration of seniors to urban centres (identified in the Idea String) implied the need for senior focused developments in rural settings. As a result, they initiated a project with the help of the Rural Alberta Development Fund to create Hunt Coulee Village, a community owned development outside the city catering to this segment of the population. It has been receiving much attention from media as well as other communities across Canada.

The proponents of the project examined all facets relating to seniors living including health care, transportation, and lifestyle. The community currently in development features a central community building with a games room, commercial kitchen and meeting rooms, shuttle service, coordinated car pooling, nature trails, greenhouse and other eco friendly features such as reduced light pollution technologies. Every home will be eco-sustainable.

The Application. Because everything has implications, anyone can benefit from the application of this IVL. Implications may be superficial. For example, they may be inherent in the language or images associated with any given idea quest. A simple exercise is to match images to language to find visual ideas for any type of communication requiring ideas. Sometimes, images inspire language.

Implications are always revealed through research. When we examine attributes, trends and shifts, these implications immediately form the Idea String. The road to uncovering implications is defined through questions. Why do we need something? Why do we behave a certain way? What happens when actions are taken? How does a quality, attribute or value affect a person, environment, system or process? If this, then what—and why? Implications.

NEGATIVE SPACE THINKING

Is negative space the space you don't like, or the space that is not there?
And if it's not there how can you tell?
—Emma Bull

In reading Emma's quote, one might further appreciate the fact that, as a science fiction and fantasy writer, she is considered to be the DNA of urban fantasy writing, which implies that she created in a world of negative space—fantasy space. This section may come across a little like science fiction, but I can assure you that Negative Space Thinking (NST) is one of the most powerful tools in the arsenal of idea generation.

I have to thank my son, Brock, a professional photographer and designer, who taught me what I know about negative space, which is, in fact, the area around a subject in a photograph. In a newspaper advertisement, it is called "white space." I extrapolated on what I learned and adapted it to develop what I refer to as "Negative Space Thinking."

It can be compared somewhat to *"outside the box"* thinking, except that NST does not have to reach beyond the borders of any particular context to connect with Inherent Values. Besides, there is nothing outside this box everyone talks about. We're always in a box of some kind. We just make the box bigger.

Just to be clear, NST does not imply that the thinking is negative or destructive. A slightly more oblique, physical example of negative space can be experienced in your own environment. Go into your living room and stand on your head. This upside down view will reveal things like available space you had not considered taking advantage of (including the ceiling). It will also reveal clutter that has accumulated more than you realized because, over time, you have become used to your room and desensitized to the long term results of your decorating quirks.

An intellectual example of NST can be found in the history book of advertising and takes us back to the latter sixties. In a bid to attract a sliver of market share from the dominant beverage brand of the day, Coca Cola, 7UP defined a USP (Unique Selling Proposition), which is iconic to advertising professionals who are old enough to remember it. 7UP's USP, which serves as a point of reference regarding strategic positioning to this very day, was proliferated throughout all media. It started as, *"It's 7UP, it's Uncola,"* and was eventually consolidated to *"7UP, the Uncola."*

It was the first time in advertising history a competitive brand used its main competitor so blatantly as a springboard to position itself. Within the context of Function-Result introduced earlier, it shows how the function of Coke as a competitor served to create a result or, more intuitively, gave meaning to the branding position of the proponent who was, in this case, 7UP.

Eyes rolled in ad agency circles around the globe. Advertising experts and pundits scoffed at the arrogance of 7UP, criticizing them for violating an advertising tenet, which stipulated that a major brand should never refer to or even compare itself to another brand in its advertising communications. It was an advertising sin, plain and simple.

The rest, as they say, is history. 7UP gained share and vaulted itself into the minds of consumers, branding themselves as an alternative. Therein is the Actionable Idea: become the alternative. 7UP recognized that, up until 1975, no one had ever challenged Coca Cola significantly as an alternative. Their research clearly indicated that consumers enjoyed variety and, as such, 7UP offered itself up as another choice. Wherein Coca Cola was the main focus—like a subject in a photograph—there was no other brand in the negative space drawing attention to itself. It was also a classic case of, *"If you want to make money, stand next to it."*

7UP did not invalidate Coca Cola's brand or position. If anything, they took advantage of the position by placing themselves right beside it. When it comes to generating ideas, this strategy can work very effectively. Sometimes, a great idea exists next to an already existing brilliant idea.

Carrying on. Another way to appreciate Negative Space Thinking is to close your eyes and listen to the world around you. If you had the opportunity to experience what blind people experience every day, it would amaze you to find out how much one doesn't hear emanating from life's activities. Even more revealing is the power of silence.

In radio, silence is referred to as "dead air." When you hear silence (an interesting contradiction in terms), it is what I describe as the loudest sound in radio broadcasting (an even more interesting contradiction in terms). Silence is to sound what negative space is to photography. I have often used silence in radio for impact. It certainly gets the listener's attention.

It is what we don't hear that speaks volumes to us. Silence in a conversation is filled with tension. We don't have to hear words to feel the drama in a relationship. If you are searching for clues to understand the issues in any relationship, listen to the silence. The search for ideas often begins in a black void and in silence. Our brain searches through our imagination for a spark, the pith of a concept. We can become easily frustrated because we feel that nothing is happening. In fact, a lot is happening. Eventually, something *occurs.* Once we initiate the creative thinking process, our brain remains busy, even when we give up.

I have learned to stop being conscious about thinking

creatively and trust my brain to do the work for me. Inevitably, something connects the dots in my brain, perhaps coached by an external occurrence like a conversation or an event I see happening and, just like that, ideas emerge.

When we stop focusing on the light, we see more in the shadows. That is the beauty of Negative Space Thinking. Forget the obvious. Look deeper inside the box rather than try to penetrate outside of it. Instead of trying to determine what someone is doing wrong, focus on what they are not doing and why they are not doing it. Also focus on what they are doing right.

When your team mates at work talk about problems, redirect the conversation to talk about opportunities and how the problems might be the departure point, the beginning of the opportunity. For example, years ago, the food retail (grocery) industry began to see less shopping carts full of groceries. It used to be that families would do their major grocery shopping once or twice a month and fill their carts. Over time, the amount of groceries in the cart kept shrinking. The problem was that families had less time to shop and were grabbing fast food more often.

On a Friday night, it was easier to order out for pizza or Chinese food at the end of a tough work week. During the week, time challenged consumers would drop in quickly after work to grab the few grocery items they absolutely needed. Food retailers grappled with the problem of shrinking purchases and searched for a solution. Then they realized that the problem was an opportunity. The answer was hiding in plain sight, but it was not where everyone was looking. They had to, in a way, stand on their marketing heads and let negative space reveal something. The Actionable Idea and the solution had already presented itself.

Grocery stores got inside their customer's lives and started offering them alternatives to fast foods: ready-to-go meals, which grew to become ready-to-go lunches and ready-to-go snacks. Consumers, who were now shopping more frequently for fewer items, found these products appealing.

Here's another example of NST. Some problems are the result of a routine that has become predictable. It is easier said than done to try and break up a routine and unilaterally dump something new into a stagnant situation. Stifled office environments infected with apathy and rife with politics are hard to change. This scenario presents a wonderful opportunity to apply NST. Doing the unexpected inspires others.

I remember working in a situation similar to the one previously described (stifled, stagnant, and inefficient). It was clear to me that offering suggestions to improve it would only be met with resistance. So, I tried a tactic that had worked for me over the years, a strategy based on a process I used regularly to get clients to buy into one of my concepts. Simply put, I made them believe it was their idea. Worked like a charm.

I modified the approach and went up to various colleagues and said, *"I heard this great idea about how we can improve our process managing clients who don't buy into our approval process and deadline issues, but I can't remember whose idea it was. Do you? It's a great idea."*

I then shared the idea and asked the colleague who they thought might have generated the idea originally. Over the next few weeks, more than one of them came back to me and more or less repeated the idea, expressing favour in implementing it. Before long, most of the team had bought into the new plan, which led to the objective I had of taking more control over a client related problem that, if left unresolved, would continue to tax our production process with inefficiencies and stress.

Perhaps even more brilliant is the fact that everyone felt they had ownership of the concept and, in fact, they did. Not only that, but, as a team, we began to believe in our collective ability to take initiatives and implement changes and new opportunities leading to greater productivity.

Negative Space Thinking is about the things we ignore around the obvious; listening to what people are saying when they don't speak; looking at things we see every day in a completely different context (upside down) and redefining that context (problem = opportunity).

Like anything, wielding NST takes practice. Try it. Stand on your head and look around. What do you see that you didn't see before? Get back on your feet. What do you see now? Negative Space Thinking (NST) is the most challenging of all the Inherent Values, but using it is always rewarding, itching us to become aware of contexts of which we are not initially aware.

In the broader sense, NST taps and stimulates intuition, because, on a subliminal level, there are ideas about reality we subvert, suppress or simply ignore. Nonetheless, they are always there, lurking in our minds. The more we apply NST, the stronger our senses become. For example, the moment we feel immediate apprehension, we have activated our intuition. Intuition is independent of any reasoning process, which means that, in order to develop NST, we have to be prepared to let go of our conventional thinking, values and judgements; not an easy thing to do. This also means we have to find the methods to trigger our minds beyond reason.

The process of engaging NST begins by asking, *"What am I not seeing?,"* and, *"What am I not hearing?"* We can approach the answers by assuming, for example, that someone means the opposite to what they are saying and examine why they would contradict themselves or simply lie.

The one thing I have always appreciated about NST is that it forces me to examine things more deeply, beginning with my own values and perceptions. NST reveals my layers of ignorance. Once exposed, it fuels my creative growth. It helps me turn, *"I don't know that which I don't know"* into, *"I know that which I don't know."*

In any relationship, we often find ourselves saying to someone else, such as a significant other, *"I don't get how you think."* This is always an opportunity to assume the opposite and define what you *do* get first. Given that the conversation has not deteriorated into a negative scuffle (and even if it does), the significant other can respond and reveal issues and perceptions, which spark enlightenment, transforming ignorance into working knowledge.

In order for NST to work at all, we have to be willing to listen, not just hear; see, not simply look; feel, not just touch, without drowning the feelings in the thinking of them. Therein is the heart and soul of NST.

Ergo: the Inherent Value of Negative Space Thinking is that it takes us to a fresh, new awareness: beyond looking to seeing, beyond hearing to listening, and beyond thinking about feelings and ideas to feeling

and being in the moment. This allows intuition to flourish through which we give meaning and generate ideas.

To set up a process of generating ideas using the Negative Space Thinking IVL, follow these steps.

Establish the Context.

- Start with the known. Describe what you clearly know about the situation breaking it down into as many aspects as possible: behaviors and attitudes, physical, functional, technical and emotional qualities and values, and the relationship users have toward the attributes.

- Separate tangible, physical aspects from philosophical, emotional and intellectual ones.

Generate the Idea String.

- List either opposites or obliquely different contexts of what you know. For example, if you have established that something is convenient to use, state what you can about how it is not convenient. My house key opens the front door. My house key does not start my car. (What if my house key opened my front door *and* started my car?)

- If something is expressed as a certainty, state the opposite. My daughter does not like to drink milk. But my daughter likes milk in her cereal. (What if the milk tasted like her cereal?)

- Find something in any arbitrarily selected image that captures any physical attributes you described within the Context. This is akin to finding faces in clouds or other images within textured surfaces.

- Turn things upside down or sideways. Write statements backwards. List procedures in reverse. (*This may seem like nonsense and, at the moment of execution, it is somewhat so. Remember, we are creating sense out of nonsense, new knowledge born within the unknown.*)

- Try to put yourself in someone else's shoes. Adopt their thinking, even if your POV does not align with theirs. Handicap yourself to experience new challenges. This process forces you to feel different behaviors, which, in turn, will affect your thought process, both consciously and subliminally. Dress opposite to your gender and go to a local watering hole. (*This would take a little bit of courage, but it is quite amazing what you will learn about the male and female persona.*)

- Switch everyone's roles at work for a day and give them full authority to do whatever is necessary (as long as it is not destructive, ridiculous, or unreasonable).

Example. The following, physical example of Negative Space Thinking comes courtesy of a wonderful artist I met in Naramata outside Kelowna in British Columbia. James Hibbert (James Hibbert Pottery) is a gifted artist creating pottery, glassware, stoneware, raku, saggarware and sculpted motifs in one of the most beautiful geographical settings in the Okanagan in British Columbia, Canada. The issue he was facing related to productivity.

The Context. Essentially, one artist can only produce so much and he was not of the disposition to employ others to help produce his art or deploy technologies to support replication. The challenge he had, the unknown he was facing, was how he might increase productivity without relying on additional resources or adding too much time to his already busy schedule, something many artists wrestle with in most categories.

The Idea String. James spent time contemplating his work to determine if there were any ways, processes or techniques to increase the production volume without sacrificing quality. As a versatile artist, his examination naturally centered itself on shapes and options within and without those shapes.

One of the most popular examples of negative space is the outline of faces we might see when looking at a vase. It is classic example of how we can see shapes within or without another shape. Visually, it looks like this.

Fig. 1

The Actionable Idea. Eventually, James focused on vases. He asked himself some *"what if"* questions. *"What if I cut the vase in half? What if I decorate the inside instead of the outside? What if I turn it from a vase into a bowl? What if I hang the bowl on the wall? These questions led me down a creative path to new designs."*

By doing so, James created two applications of the vase: one as a bowl, the other as wall mounted art. When I saw the work, I had to have it. James created these half vases such that they could be applied both ways by the owner. He attached a simple element allowing the owner the option to hang the vase shaped bowl on the wall.

James exploited the concave attribute of the bowl-shape, creating a 3-dimensional experience that is thoroughly unique. And, by implication, he doubled his productivity, invoking two bowls for every vase. Below is the piece.

Here are photos of the result. Every time I look at it, I am reminded of the power of Negative Space Thinking.

Fig. 2

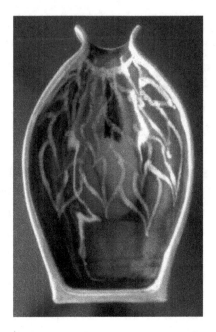

Fig 3.

The Application. The Negative Space Thinking IVL lends itself well to anything involving physical shapes and space. The leap to applying it with language is not as difficult as some may think. In language, we can look for other words embedded within other words, or even words surrounding other words within the same word.

NST reveals double entendres, hidden meanings, puns, irony, paradox, humour and various alternatives to any given POV. If you are an artist, writer, actor, director, strategist,—even a scientist—you can learn to discover the ideas hiding within the obvious. Sometimes, all it takes is breaking something apart to find a new perspective. Or, just standing on your head.

THE OTHER ALTERNATIVE

Alternative descriptions of the same reality evoke
different emotions and different associations.
—Daniel Kahneman

Daniel Kahneman, an Israeli-American psychologist, won the 2002 Nobel Memorial Prize in Economic Sciences despite the fact that he never took a single economics course. His work revealed how (as quoted by Ted.com), *". . . our 'experiencing selves' and our 'remembering selves' perceive happiness differently. This new insight has profound implications for economics, public policy—and our own self-awareness."*

Side step. In describing his book, *"The 3rd Alternative,"* in a Huffington Post article, Stephen R Covey, author and leadership authority, wrote: *"Are you willing to look for a solution that's better than what either of us have thought of?' Most people will say, 'Such as?' And you say, 'I don't know. That's the idea. Are you open to seeking a way out that's beyond your way and my way—a higher way?' That's a magic question. When your opponents see you suspend your own position, at least temporarily, suddenly the strife drains out of the discussion. Creative minds take over from antagonistic minds."*

Back step. Long before Covey published his book, I was already working with what I referred to as "the Third Alternative." It was how I defined my writer's voice: *"I see life from the edge of a coin, examining both faces to discover and explore humour, contradiction, paradox, hypocrisy, love, purpose, madness . . . everything."* I changed the name of this IVL to "The Other Alternative" out of respect for Mr. Covey's work and to avoid being perceived as a plagiarist.

The more I explored the things I wrote about, the more I realized that the edge of the coin was also a face of sorts; in effect, the Other Alternative. Answers are within rather than without. The meaning of the drill is within the function it serves and the resulting hole it creates.

An idea is not just *out there.* Ideas don't happen *after* the fact. They happen *within* the facts. They are hidden among issues, alternatives and negative space. We find ideas by hunting and gathering. After all, we are hunters and gatherers by nature. We both wait for and chase our prey, or we search for shrubs and trees to find fruit. The same thing applies to ideas. We think of the Big Idea as something that will fall into our laps out of nowhere: we think it will come to us or we will stumble upon it. Alternatives can be generated quickly by asking questions and more questions. Somewhere within the examination process, ideas will be found.

Negative Space Thinking and The Other Alternative are cousins as Inherent Values. Earlier, we examined how NST leads us to discover points of view of which we were unaware. The Other Alternative is an idea or a POV leading to another idea; an alternative inspired by the other alternatives we are considering. Sometimes, we can use Negative Space Thinking to assist us when looking for The Other Alternative.

For Steven Covey, the 3rd Alternative is "a breakthrough." From my POV, it is either a breakthrough or simply another alternative. Whichever the case, the successful application of this alternative is subject to the manifestation and execution of ideas associated with it.

If we are to alter anything, we have to consider the variations of everything from how a thing or a relationship functions to the results it produces.

Certainly, we can establish a list of desired results, which are different from the originals, but we have to account for the viability of achieving those new results. To assess viability, we have to consider the capability we have to change or vary whatever it is that will be required to generate those results.

Working backwards has its merits, which means we start with the end reel: where do we want to end up? But, what happens when we don't know where we want to end up? Even if we don't know, we can speculate on destinations and list alternatives. With everything I do, I assume there are things I do not know. I don't let it baffle or frustrate me. When I cannot visualize something, it is a trigger for me.

I respect my instincts, because my mind is telling me something at that point. It is coaching me to start looking somewhere else because the end reel in focus is a dead end, or, less harshly, it is not the place to find ideas. In client consultations, I have reeled in participants who want to give up when they hit the wall defined by the statement, *"I can't think of anything."* That's the time to use The Other Alternative IVL. Usually it begins by listing all the things tied up in a 'not,' as it were.

Ergo: the Inherent Value of The Other Alternative is that it enables us to process things in many directions: looking forward, backwards, sideways, up, down, in and out. A dead end is a direction sign, not the end of the process.

To set up a process of generating ideas using The Other Alternative IVL, follow these steps.

Establish the Context.

- This approach closely resembles that which was used for NST. Start with the known. Describe what you clearly know about the situation breaking it down into as many aspects as possible: behaviors and attitudes physical, functional, technical and emotional qualities and values, and the relationship users have toward the attributes.

- Separate tangible, physical aspects from philosophical, emotional and intellectual ones.

Generate the Idea String.

- List the most obvious alternatives. If language is at the heart of the process, list synonyms, metaphors, alternative turns of phrase or expressions communicating the same theme or concept.

- If the focus is on a physical aspect, relationship or a procedure, list the obvious alternatives beginning with the attributes and qualities. Look at them with a different POV.

- Link alternatives and examine any trends or similarities. Different combinations of alternatives will reveal implications leading to other alternatives. The implications themselves may be alternatives de facto.

Example. For years, I have been working with Sobeys, one of Canada's largest food retailers. They also own Safeway Canada. My role in more recent years as a subcontractor to their contracted Creative Producer,

Danny Cole, has been to generate themes, concepts and creative material for their annual retailer's conference.

The Context. Every year, Sobeys looks for a conference theme, which embraces the context of their marketing vision for the upcoming year. For this particular year, the retail giant had established a new agreement with its retailers, invoking a new wrinkle within the status quo of their business relationships. The implication was to strengthen these relationships moving forward within a highly competitive industry.

On the heels of various themes already generated, the Sobeys review committee asked us to go back to the drawing board. The selected theme at the time, "Partners In Action," fell from grace when it was decided that the phrase might be negatively misinterpreted as "Partners Inaction" when expressed out loud.

The Idea String. Using one of my favorite techniques for generating alternatives, especially in language, I tabled a new list of suggestions. It started with a trip to Google where I searched various keyword strings such as "partnerships," "partners," "taking action," "partners in success," and "partnership agreements." The search included quotes and sayings relating to these keyword phrases and terms. Then I trolled through synonym dictionaries focusing on such terms as "partners," "partnerships," "success," and "action."

The Actionable Idea. The final list of suggestions looked like the following. It included limited rationale for each one. Note: each theme is an Actionable Idea.

- **Partners In Motion**
  Images/analogies of anything in motion: athletes,

teams playing, relay race exchanges, vehicles, tornadoes: conference can include exercises that couple intellectual and physical activities; team activities

- **A Partnership of Possibilities**
  A theme around optimism and meeting challenges together: Sub theme: Impossible—I'm Possible (Which is copyright to me)

- **Collaboration (20XX)**
  This is an alternative to 'partnership.' Themes can focus on collaborative messages and exercises etc. Suggests a 'working together' culture

- **Taking Action Together**
  Repositioning 'action' to avoid the initial issue they had with the phrase.

- **Taking Action In Partnership**
  A version of the previous with partnership.

- **The League of Extraordinary Partners**
  Lends itself to creativity around super heroes.

- **An Active Partnership**
  Suggests a current reality.

- **Active Partners**
  Version of previous.

- **The Partnership Connection**
  Theme suggests how everyone connects; implies a positive connection. Images, symbols etc. about people connecting and getting things done; achieving success through a positive connection.

- **A Greater Partnership**
  Suggests forward momentum and growth.

- **Partners Today and Tomorrow**
  Implies the optimism of currency and the future,
  sustainability, consistency; focuses on real and long-
  term relationships.

- **The Partnership Equation (20XX)**
  Implies a definition of what comprises success.

- **People. Products. Profit. Partnership.**
  "The 4Ps of Success" might be the byline.

- **Action Through Partnership**
  Another spin on 'action.'

- **Working Together**
  Simple, but suggests collaboration, intention, and
  commitment.

- **Together: A Powerful Team**
  Self explanatory.

- **The Power of Two**
  Somewhat indirect and more of a metaphorical
  context.
  Implies a powerful 'team' and 'relationship' as well as
  exponential potential.

- **Work Together. Grow Together. Succeed together.**
  Alternate form: **Work. Grow. Succeed. Together.**
  The triptych thing. Also provides for
  compartmentalization of topics and materials during
  the conference. How do we work together? How do
  we grow? Succeed?

  The Application. Which one would you pick? Sobeys'
choice will be revealed shortly.

For anyone engaged in writing (especially advertising, articles, web content, reports, and essays) or theme development involving language for promotions, activations or events, The Other Alternative IVL is highly potent.

Google Analytics, specifically as it relates to rankings of keywords and keyword phrases, is a tool providing a highly relevant scope of alternatives, enabling writers (in fact everyone) to find ideas quickly. If you know little or nothing about Search Engine Optimization and you still want to improve your web content, all you need in your arsenal is a little understanding of Google Analytics and keyword rankings to take a significant step forward toward achieving better search results.

Another way to apply The Other Alternative is to reverse engineer your situation. List everything step by step from where you are to where you started. List alternatives you might have considered for each step and speculate on the outcome. At some point, you will begin to see issues you did not see before revealed through the alternatives. These alternatives can also generate concepts for innovation.

Alternatives can be generated by simply stating the opposite to anything on your list. The key to finding thought provoking alternatives is to *alter* the known with reckless abandon.

And now, the moment you were waiting for. Sobeys choice: **Work Together. Grow Together. Succeed together.**

PROXIMITY INFLUENCE

(*If You Want to Make Money, Stand Next to It*)

Our minds influence the key activity of the brain, which then influences everything; perception, cognition, thoughts and feelings, personal relationships; they're all a projection of you.
—Deepak Chopra

Despite the controversy around the principles expounded by Deepak Chopra, author, speaker and physician, his belief in the power of influence has touched millions. According to him, our minds have a direct influence on our physical state to the point of healing.

Influence on our own perceptions and those of others have been a hot topic for other iconic figures such as Napolean Hill who wrote, *"Think twice before you speak, because your words and influence will plant the seed of either success or failure in the mind of another."*

I have been fascinated for years trying to understand the power of influence, watching the behaviors of devoted fans around their gurus. It was also interesting to watch people use their proximity to influence and advance their own agendas, paying particular attention to how individuals projected themselves using the influence of others more powerful.

This is the context within which I developed the Proximity Influence IVL, the goofy, younger sister to the By Implication IVL. The difference is that, by applying this value, we *create* implication. It is not always organically inherent. We derive implications within the circumstances we find ourselves in, which can be unusual, often humorous and ironic. Put another way, an idea can also be found or discovered standing next to another idea; hence, my metaphorical sub-title, *"If you want to make money, stand next to it."*

Walt Disney, father to Mickey Mouse and the creative genius who drove the development of the animated film genre, believed in his ideas with unreserved confidence; in a word, implicitly. He said, *"When you believe in a thing, believe in it all the way, implicitly and unquestionable."* He too, believed in the power of the mind to influence outcomes. Even more significant is how he transformed the world of imaginary characters and fantasy experiences into a reality. Disneyland, created in 1955, is still among the top family attractions today.

His inspiration to create Disneyland came after visiting several amusements parks with his daughters. He found the idea for Disneyland by marrying two separate concepts standing next to each other: amusement parks and the animated world he created. When he recognized that the two ideas could stand together, the implication of a *theme* park, not just an amusement park, was invoked—and the rest is *his* story.

To illustrate how we create implications in everyday life, the following examples will be helpful. Picture a man whose style and appearance is such that he does not attract significant attention. Now, imagine a very attractive, stunning, woman standing next to him, her arm in his. The cliché perception? Inquiring minds are asking, *"Wonder who that guy is to attract such a beauty?"* The implication is created in their minds that he is someone special, perhaps a wealthy or important individual (as is often the assumption). Simply put, perceptions are created through a misconstrued implication. His proximity to her influences the perceptions of others.

Another snapshot. At a business function, a business woman stands next to another business woman. One of them is a well known, highly respected CEO of a large corporation. The woman standing next to her is unknown and has the CEO engaged in a highly animated conversation. The unknown woman is definitely making an impression on the CEO. The body language between the two of them implies familiarity. Implication? Assumptions are made that the unknown woman must be a mover and shaker in business. Inquiring minds want to know who the unknown woman is and make efforts throughout the remainder of the function to connect with her.

Yet another snapshot already examined earlier. In the late 60's, 7UP described itself as an Uncola in a massive advertising campaign and attracted consumers to 7UP as an alternative choice in the beverage market. In effect, 7UP stood next to Cola to get the attention and the engagement—and earned significant market share in the process. 7UP blatantly created the implication. It was not until the campaign ran that consumers considered 7UP as an alternative.

Ideas, like organisms, can be symbiotic and exist interdependently. When we examine one thing or idea, we can discover, through its attributes and values, the triggers for other ideas that are linked to the first idea. This kind of creative thinking is typical of painters, especially those who look at the images of reality and capture them as an abstract, a representation of what we see in a form that begins to define itself.

Picasso, the iconic Spanish, Cubist painter, comes to

mind. He said, *"There is no abstract art. You must always start with something. Afterward you can remove all traces of reality."* Picasso's perspective echoes those of sculptors who will tell you that they carve away the material (rock or wood) to *reveal* the statue or figure within, which implies that the figure already exists. This was certainly the view held by Michelangelo. In some ways, the same can be said for ideas, which can be revealed when we peel away the things we know, both obvious and implied.

To sit in a room staring at the ceiling and trying to come up with an idea usually leads to staring a little longer at the ceiling until we give up. To repeat: we *find* ideas. We live in the present, to which we give meaning. Even when we stumble upon ideas, it requires our stumbling to find them. Wherein some implications originate from pre-existing circumstances, Proximity Influence constitutes implications we create. Put another way, if you want to enhance the value of something, stand next to something similar that already has an established value. (To repeat: if you want to make money, stand next to it.)

It is a simple two-step process. Find something—person, thing, symbol, language—that is highly recognizable and has value. Define direct and indirect ways to associate with it. There's the recipe. An association can be created visually, such as featuring the logos of important clients on your website to imply the high quality of your product or service.

An implied association can be created through language. For example, a retailer can offer an "unconditional guarantee" on their products, which implies a commitment to quality, which is more effective than just stating something like, *"We believe in quality."*

In order to invoke a sense of quality, the company takes a position (stands next to) a policy addressing quality assurance that is absolute by definition as well as highly recognizable.

Over the years, my colleagues at a live events production company have booked big name music acts and celebrities to perform or appear at the annual Christmas Party, including Bret Michaels (Poison), Ruben Studdard (American Idol), Chip Coffey (A&E Paranormal State), Kim Mitchell (Canadian rock legend) and several others. The result was that the production company earned a reputation for being incredibly 'cool and progressive.' They had no trouble attracting record numbers to their production warehouse and, by implication, word of mouth spread in the community, enhancing the company's brand.

Auto manufacturers vie for a favourable nod from J.D. Powers, the creator of the blue chip, customer satisfaction and product quality recognition program. It's all about brands standing next to brands to enhance the value of the lesser known brand.

Driving a certain type of vehicle will create perceptions about the driver. Living in a certain neighbourhood characterizes the resident. A quote from someone recognized as an expert will enhance the value and credibility of your own idea. Testimonials from respected individuals will further validate your credibility and value. And so it goes. Ultimately, we can create implications through association. It is not always easy, but it is always possible.

Ergo: the Inherent Value of Proximity Influence is that it creates implications by design through

influence and association, particularly with strong, recognizable brands. The context of 'brand' can be anything from a person to a recognizable symbol or logo.

To set up a process of generating ideas using the Proximity Influence IVL, follow these steps.

Establish the Context.

- Generally speaking, a situation calling for the application of the Proximity Influence IVL is associated with a need to establish, build or strengthen credibility, brand positioning, relationships, products, services or key messages, which can benefit from strong, well established and recognizable influences. The simplest form of Proximity Influence is endorsement, but when it is difficult to secure one, the next best thing is to *imply* endorsement.

Generate the Idea String.

- List symbols including logos, as well as images, certifications, awards, individuals, organizations, companies or anything that associates with your context, especially those with which you have a connection through various relationships. These may be clients or important projects. List both current and past associations.

- If your situation involves a key message, such as a policy statement or some other strategic message, research the writings, interviews and speeches of well known individuals (authors, politicians, philosophers, business and cultural leaders) who have made clear and compelling statements, which link to your message. Students can certainly benefit from this process. Too often, I have read essays with arguments lacking support, relying only on an individual POV and rationale.

Example. Radio is one of the most challenging mediums when it comes to creating memorable commercials. Without the benefit of visuals, the objective is to stimulate the listener's experience by triggering mental images through sound and language.

Sometimes, producers will overwhelm the message with sound effects, stingers, over-the-top characters and dialogue in an effort to break through the clutter. In this example, I relied on a single voice and leveraged the public's awareness of something, specifically a personality, who already had profile and a high level of awareness.

The Context. An automotive dealership I have worked with over the years relies heavily on radio to brand itself, although radio is not considered to be the strongest medium for branding. Rather, it is used to drive promotion with strong calls to action. However, in this case, we had successfully used radio to create brand awareness. (See Case Study #11 later in this book.)

A good friend and colleague of mine, Gord Marriott, is a talented voice artist and performs several celebrity impressions. The issue is that, although impressionists are permitted to perform voice-a-likes in live performances without requiring the permission of the celebrity (referred to as legal infringement of copyright, which protects an artist's right to perform a parody), the same does not apply to advertising. In other words, in a radio commercial, someone cannot portray a celebrity and be identified as being that celebrity by name. This would be considered a fake endorsement.

The Idea String. One of Gord's characters is reminiscent of a well known actor who also does voiceovers for an international brand. But in order to keep it legal, we could not identify the real actor or use language that was similar to the copy being used in that brand's campaign. So we explored ways to modify the character and the language to avoid any issues. I generated a description of several personalities based on the characteristics associated with this particular style of voice: redneck and cowboy. I also researched cowboy slang and linked it to messages associated with the dealership. The foundation was established and we went to work.

The Actionable Idea. One format not being used by the international brand in their advertising was the application of dialogue with another character or personality. So, the scripts I developed manifested various dialogues between the dealer principal and the character portrayed by Gord. The attitude of Gord's character was defined very clearly: he tolerated the dealer principal, but never ignored the opportunity to rattle his chain. The end result was a radio campaign that achieved significant awareness. Listeners knew that the voice was not that of the actual actor. At best, it was similar and, most importantly, it was legal.

We have continued to develop scripts for this redneck cowboy who has taken on a life of his own. As a soft parody of the real actor's character, the campaign itself has become a parody within advertising.

The Application. If credibility, branding and positioning is on your agenda, the Proximity Influence IVL makes life simple. As a business with a website, you can tell a powerful story by featuring the recognizable logos of some of your more notable clients.

In terms of endorsement, even if you do not have access to a tier one celebrity, you can always establish a relationship with someone credible in your community to support your efforts. Factual and honest testimonials are worth their weight in gold.

Too often, inexperienced advertisers fall into the trap of making direct statements such as, *"We have knowledgeable and friendly staff who care about you, the customer."* The problem is most consumers today bemoan the poor level of service and lack of knowledge they encounter; however, when they hear that message from other customers, it leverages and drives the message home with greater impact, credibility and integrity.

For intellectual applications, positioning your message next to a strong metaphor or image, sometimes both, can invoke the influence you need in order to get the attention from your audience or target market. Association is a powerful tool. Who or what do you need to stand next to find the ideas you are looking for?

ATTITUDE—ALTITUDE

Your attitude, not your aptitude, will determine your altitude.
—Zig Ziglar

Salesman and motivational icon, Zig Ziglar, truly exemplified the notion and meaning inherent in his famous quote, which implies that we can achieve whatever we believe regardless of our experience or circumstances.

Earl Nightingale (The Strangest Secret), Deepak Chopra (The Book of Secrets), Tony Robbins (Unlimited Power), Napoleon Hill (Think and Grow Rich), Abraham Hicks (Law of Attraction) and many others have all said similar things. The reason they became iconic has more to do with the fact that we—their audiences and readers—believed in what they said about our own potential as human beings. At the very least, we *wanted* to believe in what they were saying. It has been a journey for me to truly act on what I believed was possible for myself. Nonetheless, slowly, over the years, my dreams have become actualized through effort and a little luck—and a little dose of Nightingale, Robbins *et al.*

Most mornings, I look into a large mirror hanging next to the front door of my house and, regardless of how I feel, I tell the guy in the mirror that I will have an awesome day; that I am going to achieve something valuable, no matter how small, which will take me closer to realizing my goals and dreams. No matter how lethargic or stressed I feel, I force myself to do it. It is a regular psychological and motivational churning designed to convert fantasies into dreams, dreams into goals and goals into action. Results are inevitable—positive or negative—but all good.

If you were to do the same thing and state with resolve that you will generate a brilliant idea relating to whatever quest you are pursuing, it will happen. If your skepticism still prevails as you read this, I get it. Remember this. You *are* reading this book. Somewhere within the skeptic you, there is an optimistic and motivated person reaching out for something more. The process you are engaged in right now is the evidence of your potential.

Rewind. As children, we are imprinted with attitudes, behaviors, mannerisms, beliefs and values through the experiences we have with our parents, siblings, relatives, friends, teachers and those we perceive to be heroes, real and fictitious. We are conditioned and influenced throughout our lifetime.

Our response to this conditioning evolves and, certainly, we take more control of its effect as we grow older; however, as children, we are much more vulnerable and receptive to the influences around us. How we sound when we speak, the cadence of our speech, the way we walk, laugh, what we think is funny, sad, good, evil—it all starts as imprints.

Sometime around the time we turn eight and nine, our own individual sense of identity begins to take shape. Then, as teenagers, the biological clock hard wires us to a greater sense of purpose and meaning in our lives, which is why we challenge the rules, and experiment with our bodies and minds in secret places. Pretty creative stuff, too. Eventually we start to figure out what works and doesn't work, rejecting some things and getting addicted to others.

Within all this, our creativity is also shaped. As children, we watch important figures in our life invoke creativity as they generate ideas for everything from party themes to Halloween costumes. We also watch them deal with problems as they try to find solutions—to right wrongs, fix relationships, reconfigure the backyard flower bed—*ad nauseum.*

We continue to learn and grow until we die. We learn about creativity every second we breathe. Ideas are generated with every breath we take. Regardless, many of us allow our creativity to become limited by or buried under the pressures of surviving. So, how do we re-ignite or turn up the creative flame?

My ignition switch is the same one I used as a child. I adopt a character with behaviors and attitudes just for shitz and giggles. For example, I pretend, to this day, that I am the most sought after creative thinker, the object of media attention and public demand. I imagine myself being interviewed for a documentary about me. Yes, this is all intensely selfish and, perhaps, a little egotistical. Fun, too, especially when no one is watching. I never question the depth of my expertise or passion.

The interview questions range from how I experienced creativity as a child to how it evolved and what changed along the way. The questions are always probing. Who are my biggest influences? What do I intend to achieve with my creativity? Eventually, all of this pretending ramps up to a specific question, which is at the heart of something I need an idea for.

So, what the heck am I doing? By adopting an attitude that assumes a level of confidence in my creativity, I subliminally break up the cobwebs that normally stifle the creative thinking process. It is important to note that

I am also using the game of pretending, which, for most of us when we were children, stimulated the highest level of creative thinking. At this point, I have no explanation other than to say that ideas simply start to flow. Whatever it is inside the brain that connects these dots, it is actively stimulating creative thoughts and ideas.

Back to you. Let's assume you are part of a team at your place of work, engaged in a project that requires ideas. Try this exercise.

- Assume you are in that important meeting at the point where you just presented the actionable idea. Never mind that you don't actually have the idea yet.

- Fast forward to a scenario in which you have been asked to report to one of the top people in your company who wants to speak with you regarding your brilliant idea.

- Imagine you are in their office and they ask you about how you generated the idea. Describe the process.

- What was the established agenda?

- Who was assembled and why?

- How did the discussion begin?

- Outline what specific issue required an idea and what kind of idea you were searching for, such as a solution idea, a new approach idea, a theme idea, a headline idea—whatever works in your industry or situation.

- Describe the strategy that was developed to generate the idea.

- If research was required, describe the scope of research.

- Describe the various conversations that took place to define the situation. Talk about everything except the idea (because, at this point, the idea has not revealed itself).

- Every once in a while, imagine that the person listening to you is responding with kudos for the milestones that occurred during the meeting. Let the emphasis of this acknowledgment be on you.

- Allow yourself to enjoy your new found stardom and bask in the limelight. The company owes you big time for the significant result you contributed to, so let it in. Smell that promotion

The deeper you allow yourself to engage in this personal role play, the sooner you will spark ideas that will be actionable. Attitude, among other manners and dispositions, will change or, at least, tip how your brain thinks and processes. In some ways, you trick yourself into believing in yourself (again) and, by doing so, you release the natural, creative persona that has always been inside you, the persona that has always been there.

You have to step outside your constant, grinding reality to access it, which, with enough practice, you will find you can do most of the time. Life isn't perfect and life always intervenes without a calling card. If you are so inclined, you can perform this exercise with someone else who you trust and feel comfortable with.

Just because you grew up doesn't mean you have to leave behind everything you did freely as a child. In fact, your imagination and creativity have developed and evolved, but, perhaps, you haven't been exercising it lately. Somewhere buried under the layers of life—under the tenet that adults do not engage in childhood games on their own—is a playful, spirited imp begging to be allowed out. It is time to enjoy life with childlike, reckless abandon. Recognizing that it is not always easy to give oneself permission to be silly, this is your invitation to find the means and ways to unleash the individual within you who enjoys making stuff up and altering reality.

Try this. On any work day, dress in a manner that is completely inconsistent with your work environment. For example, if you work in an industrial or warehouse setting, perhaps in the office area where you usually dress in casual attire, dress yourself spanky instead, as long as it doesn't interfere with your duties or violate regulations. Wear an outfit that is tailored. Walk in to work making a fashion statement. (Guys, please remember to polish your shoes.)

Make up a story that you are going to a special event after work, so that your outfit is justified. For those of you who dress for a more formal setting, such as a legal office, augment your dress code even more, or radically change the style within parameters that, even if they flirt with a little notoriety, are reasonably acceptable in that environment.

Spend the day doing what you normally do and enjoy the reactions you get from people who have never seen you dressed in this manner. More importantly, notice the changes in your own behavior. For some of your colleagues, the variances may be more subtle. Whatever the level of the response, it will affect you. There is more to observe in this cause and effect scenario stimulated by an alternate attitude.

Notice how you feel and how your experience inside a predictable routine transforms. You will become highly sensitized to the social interaction, as will your colleagues. Notice also how it affects your thinking, imagination and, ultimately, your attitude and disposition. These effects will impact your creativity and spark the idea engine. When we feel differently, we think differently and we shed some of the usual behaviors, if only for the moment. Although it is somewhat force-fed, we become hard-wired to a different experience, an altered state as it were, and, often, it is exhilarating. A change in feelings and real perspective is one of the strongest mechanisms to enhance our intellectual and creative sensibilities.

Side step. "Suspension of disbelief." This is a term referring to our disposition to become emotionally engaged when watching a theatre play, movie or television show. We suspend our disbelief that the story is not real and give ourselves permission to embrace it.

We did it as children and we do it as adults. This is a very powerful altered state. It also links us directly to our imaginations, so much so, we are capable of crying for those suffering in a dramatic story. We welcome an altered state of truth—a fabricated truth. Viscerally, we embed ourselves in the surrounding intellectual and emotional mass of that fabricated truth. It is one of the most profound, creative things our species is capable of doing.

Side step again. In the real world, we all tell stories about ourselves. They began with a real event. Something happened. And then, we keep talking about it. If we track back through our lives, we can identify moments such as the first time we recognized something was wrong and never wanted it to happen again, the first time we didn't feel connected to a group, in fact, that we didn't belong, and the first time we decided we would do it on our own and became independent. These stories evolve throughout life. How much do they change? Some stories never change. Many more do. If a story had its DNA in trauma, it most likely changes because we would rather not remember the trauma. Regardless, we carry the pain and it affects our behavior, especially our relationships.

Over time, the details become smudged, altered, amplified, twisted, turned and sautéed. This does not imply that the story becomes inaccurate. If the story's origin was a happy one, perhaps even a triumphant one, it may get embellished more and more. Notice how a couple in love keeps building on the story about the time they got engaged or had their first child.

In some ways, we suspend disbelief even within our own story of life. Sometimes, it is easier to believe the story we tell, rather than the story that actually happened. Does this reflect a lack of integrity? No. It makes us human. What it also says is that we are highly creative when it comes to how our mind survives the emotional and intellectual adventures we wander through in life.

The inspiration for Attitude-Altitude as an Inherent Value came from Zig Ziglar's quote, *"Your attitude, not your aptitude, will determine your altitude.,"* cited earlier in this book. It always bears repeating.

Creatively, many of us are trapped in low attitudes, which keep us at low altitudes, despite our aptitude. The experience in a roomful of people at a think tank or meeting, where ideas are being generated, can be daunting or frustrating for the individuals who are either concerned about suggesting something for fear of being ineffective or for those who are comfortable sharing ideas but don't know where to start owing to issues in the situation. Anything from politics to a lack of understanding will always stifle creativity.

When the goal is to generate Actionable Ideas, the collective attitude is just as important to respect as the individual attitudes in the room. Attitudes do not have to align perfectly for a group to process creatively and productively. Attitudes need to be understood or, at the very least, accepted, which sets up for a group attitude channelled through collaboration. Diversity of opinion and points-of-view are assets, not liabilities. Diversity spawns diversely brilliant ideas.

Ergo: the Inherent Value of Attitude -Altitude is that it alters and shifts points of view, individually and collectively, leading to a discovery of more attributes (qualities), and meanings (values), which trigger Actionable Ideas.

To set up a process of generating ideas using the Attitude—Altitude IVL, follow these steps.

Establish the Context.

- Describe the situation and identify what aspects of the situation are affected by the attitudes of those associated with it.

- Describe the attitudes and points of view (POVs), including your own, associated with the situation.

Generate the Idea String.

- List causes that may be triggering various POVs.

- Examine the attitudes to determine any trends, similarities or conflicts between them.

- State alternate attitudes and see how these variations can affect the situation as well as how it may affect other POVs.

Example. When I was contracted to work with William Shatner on his live show, I was—well—blown away. Here was my opportunity to put my creative process to work with an international icon of television and film. Instantly I wondered what it would be like to work with someone of his stature. What kind of attitudes would come into play and how would they affect the show we were creating? I was going to find out.

The Context. William Shatner was preparing to mount a live tour in Canada based on his autobiographical book, "How Time Flies." It was to be a two-man show involving Canadian broadcaster, Alan Cross, who would engage Mr. Shatner in an on-stage conversation about his life, career and philosophies. The discussion would be supported by visuals including photographs, text, and clips from television and film. The challenge I faced was to boil down a daunting amount of information about this man's life into a two and a half hour theatrical experience.

The Idea String. This is a story about a change in attitude—mine—and how it would affect the creative process. We first met Mr. Shatner in his office in Los

Angeles. Following the brief meet and greet, we sat down in his office around a coffee table to discuss the project. To say I was nervous is an understatement. So, I sat quietly and listened carefully as everyone outlined the task at hand. Mr. Shatner had mounted a similar show in Australia, but he was not completely satisfied with the structure. Ahhh. A problem requiring a solution.

As the conversation continued, I became more aware of my own silence. The inner voice was whining. *"Say something, you idiot!"* With all of my creative experience and ideation techniques, I was a deer in the headlights.

To gather my thoughts, I decided to try as best I could to imagine that Mr. Shatner was not famous; that he was just a man with an interesting story. So, I listened to his story and how he told it, all the while reminding myself that I had earned the opportunity to be in this room. Most importantly, I listened to how he talked about ideas. Something interesting emerged.

I realized he and I expressed ourselves creatively in very similar ways. Perhaps it was no accident. He was from Montreal where he performed in theatre and radio, just as I had. His Father was a Jewish immigrant, as was mine. He went to Toronto to establish his career as a performer, as I did. He made it to New York and went on to become famous. I went to Fort McMurray, Alberta. So much for parallels. Realizing these interesting coincidences, I decided that he and I were similar artistically and that it was the right time and the right place for me to offer what I could at this creative forum. Finally, I raised my hand. *"I have an idea."*

The Actionable Idea. The idea was to compartmentalize the show in a sequence that would allow him to bounce around spontaneously if he wanted to, allowing him to feel engaged at all times during the performance as opposed to always slaving to a sequence. The room fell silent. He looked at me with an intensity he has always been known for. *"That's a great idea."* (I wish I could say it took 60 seconds and perhaps I might justify that by assuming the process was triggered once I changed my *attitude*.)

The story doesn't end there. I was now back in my writer's den exchanging long phone conversations with him. After spending countless hours boiling down his life story into a number of sections, I submitted the first draft of the show. He wasn't completely impressed. *"I have concerns,"* he said. For a moment, panic percolated within me, but, once again, I reminded myself that I deserved to be in this hot seat and could handle it. So, I hit the attitude throttle again. This time, I put myself in Mr. Shatner's shoes and considered his POV. I knew that, from his POV, he needed to know that the creative process was under control. This, I concluded, would be something I would want to know, if it were my story.

So I reassured him that, with an understanding of his concerns, I now had a better reference to his thinking, which could be applied to the second draft. Subsequently, the second draft met with much more success and the rest is history, or, perhaps, more accurately—*his* story.

The Application. No matter who you are or what you do, your attitude contributes to all aspects of creativity. The realization of an Actionable Idea depends on the attitudes of those involved in the execution of it. By changing my attitude within the Shatner paradigm, I was able to actively listen and really hear what mattered to which I responded creatively, contributing to the Idea String in a meaningful way.

When you find yourself drifting during a meeting, especially one involving creative discussions, focus on your attitude and consider what may be affecting it. If you need to refocus on the task at hand, zone in on the attitudes and POVs around you. Get outside of yourself. It will help you clear the cobwebs and filters to the degree that allows your creative process to breathe.

The same thing applies to relationships. If something is missing, take the time to assess the POVs and attitudes. All the ideas in the world will amount to little if the attitudes are not understood or aligned. If your attitude is such that you do not believe you are creative nor have any ideas to offer, then that is exactly the reality you will experience. I can't quote Mr. Nightingale enough. *"You become what you think about."*

SHITZ & GIGGLES

Most discoveries even today are a combination
of serendipity and of searching.
—Siddhartha Mukherjee

Shitz & Giggles itches creativity. And a good scratch releases the most serendipitous ideas.

In work performed in his lab with collaborators in the 1990s and 2000s, Siddhathra Mukherjee, physician, scientist and Pulitzer Prize winning author (The Emperor of All Maladies: A Biography of Cancer), identified genes and chemicals that can alter the microenvironment and the behaviour of normal stem cells and cancer cells, a discovery which has had a significant impact on the development of effective treatments for cancer.

Research and experimentation coupled with accidents, happenstances and serendipitous moments have led humanity to stumble upon world changing ideas. The honor role includes:

- Alexander Bell and the telephone, when, at the moment he called for his assistant Watson for help, the vibration of the diaphragm caused a needle to vibrate in the water in which it was placed and Watson heard Bell clear as a—well—bell

- Ruth Wakefield and the chocolate chip cookie, when, after running out of baker's chocolate, she substituted chunks of sweetened chocolate thinking the chunks would melt, which they didn't

- Richard Jones, a naval engineer who, while trying to develop a meter to monitor power on naval ships, dropped a tension spring, which kept bouncing, inadvertently creating the Slinky

- A cook by the name of Crum and the potato chip, which he accidently created when a dissatisfied customer demanding thinner potatoes kept sending them back until, in a fury, Crum cut them extremely thin and fried them until they were completely hard

- An unknown Chinese cook and fireworks, invented as a result of an accident involving a mixture of charcoal, sulfur, and saltpeter (common ingredients in Chinese kitchens 2000 years ago), which, when compressed in a bamboo tube, exploded.

The list is long, including X-rays, the microwave, the heart pacemaker, Silly Putty, Scotchguard, Corn Flakes, Viagara, Post-it notes, and even the inkjet printer.

Ideas, like inventions, happen by design and by accident. They can occur spontaneously and randomly. When the last thing we are focusing on is to find an idea, at that moment, an idea happens. The unexpected idea is just as wonderful an experience in the realization of it as is the idea derived through a process applying Inherent Values. However, it is unpredictable, undependable, inconsistent and unreliable.

As much as I respect and appreciate those creative professionals who have developed ideation techniques based on accidental or random contexts, I prefer to work with a more tangible, creative process, which delivers relevant results (ideas) more predictably. This is particularly important in situations involving branding strategies. It is also critical to a committee of inexperienced people who are assembled to generate anything that involves creative rationale for such things as an event, or a strategic outcome such as a solution to a problem. In other words, ideas generated through Inherent Values stand up to scrutiny and accountability more readily than those invoked through more radical, unpredictable creative approaches.

My inclusion of a more free-form IVL may appear to be a contradiction in terms. It is not. The process of generating brilliant ideas every 60 seconds functions best when the IVLs are allowed to work together. Shitz & Giggles is part of the family, and the family that plays together, generates ideas together. Notwithstanding this inclusion, S&G can be used exclusively if the situation allows for it.

In the realm of random idea generation, there are many techniques out there, which work reasonably well, some better than others. I am simply adding my flavour to the mix, recognizing that some techniques may appear similar to others already established. At the heart of these are the exercises that begin with singular words, phrases, symbols or images. If there is anything to be added, it is the sequence in which these things occur.

What I like about these thought-starter techniques is the fact that any aspect of language (word, phrase, symbol or image) does not have to be intrinsically relevant to the main topic or objective for which an idea is being sought. In fact, the less relevant they are, the greater the chance of stimulating the Idea String that may lead, albeit accidently, to the desired result.

How I maintain the integrity of my approach, even within the accidental context, is by including aspects of the IVLs I have covered in this chapter. At the end of the day, my version of ideation is one of many. As one who believes in competitive transparency, I invite everyone to reach out to engage other established idea generating processes, because they all have their own merit. The more the merrier, I say. In fact, to engage in different processes can only lead to an even greater unleashing of your creativity.

Robert David Steele, American activist, former Central Intelligence Agency clandestine services case officer and author of "The Open-Source Everything Manifesto: Transparency, Truth, and Trust," wrote, *"Transparency, which engenders truth, is the foundation for all this."* Despite Steele's intentions with his message, "all this" currently lives in a darker world. Still, I share his optimism for a better world, which, for me, means one that can be healed, calmed and inspired by ubiquitous, robust, rigorous and unbridled creativity. Ideas solve problems, create opportunities, and transform lives. To borrow a thought in part from Shakespeare, all the world should be on that stage.

John Cleese, one of the brilliant, original founders of Monty Python's Flying Circus, a British comedy group made famous through their zany sketches on television as well feature films, said in a Video Arts lecture, *"Creativity is not a talent. It is not a talent, it is a way of operating."* The full transcript is worth reading. http://news.rapgenius.com/John-cleese-lecture-on-creativity-annotated.

When we become less aware of life's circumstances or find ourselves in casual situations feeling less inhibited, our creativity comes up to the surface. We don't evaluate it, linger on strategy, mire ourselves in objectives—we just do it without any reason except to have fun. That's who we really are, until we are sucked back deeper into the box of reality as we see it.

Creativity is a way of operating. The process can be strategic (as it is within this book) or it can be random, spontaneous, non-linear and devoid of highly regimented guidelines. So, for those of you who think that creative people are talented, then this is your chance to realize that *anyone* can operate creatively. It is an important distinction to make because we undermine our creativity by defining it as talent.

In a workshop in Los Angeles, I had one hour to generate brilliant ideas for a group of about 40 entrepreneurs. There wasn't a lot of time, so I decided to go with a very random, no-frills, creative exercise to get things going. To start, I asked the room if anyone needed an idea for anything. The eager candidate, a solar panel retailer, jumped in and stated his case, which I will expand on in the case study section. Once I understood the context and had the background to his story, I asked the room, for shitz and giggles, to generate one word or short phrase ideas—the first thing that came to their minds, whether it was relevant or not. Sixty seconds later, we had a list.

I scanned the list and picked the first thing that got my attention. I had an idea in 30 seconds. Then, it became interesting. A man in the front row put up his hand. He had an idea. He was followed by a woman at the back, then, another woman on the other side of the room. It kept going.

By the end of the session, we had collectively generated almost a dozen ideas, some of which led to ideas for others. A participant came up to me as I was about to make my exit and said, *"That was the most amazing thing I've seen in a long time."* It felt good to hear. It does every time. I've seen it hundreds of times. It still amazes me. If I know anything, our creativity knows how to operate, especially when we step out of the way. When we forget about trying to figure out how we're going to come up with ideas, we find them and generate them quickly. Talent does not define creativity.

Ergo: the Inherent Value of Shitz & Giggles is the creative freedom it provides. It distracts us from preconceived notions and allows the process of idea generation to be organic. Results are inevitable.

To set up a process of generating ideas using the Shitz & Giggles IVL, follow these steps.

Establish the Context.

- Describe the situation and state the objective. Keep it as simple as possible.

- If it is a multi-faceted problem or situation, break it down into clearly defined components. Think in terms of singularities.

Generate the Idea String. (NOTE: this is just one, selected technique.)

- For each component, randomly list as many words, symbols and images as you can. There is no requirement for any of these to be directly associated to the situation or objective. (*I often suggest that people list the first things that come to mind without analyzing it.*)

- If you are working with a group, set a very short time limit (like 60 seconds) so as to create a sense of urgency and minimize over-analysis.

- Draw relationships or connections between all of the elements .listed paying close attention to any implications that may emerge.

- Connect these relationships and implications to the situation and objective and articulate a rationale. Feel free to bend and twist the rationale.

Example. Throughout the course of writing this book,

I have often found myself engulfed in conversations about ideation. The experience of the following application of the Shitz & Giggles IVL occurred in under ten seconds. Somehow, in hindsight, it makes me appreciate the genius of the late Robin Williams who said, "*No matter what people tell you, words and ideas can change the world.*"

The Context. At a barbeque gathering, a woman with whom I was having a conversation with about my book challenged me to "come up" with a brilliant idea in 60 seconds. She was planning to attend a costume party with a casino theme and needed a concept for a costume and didn't want to wear something predictable like a card dealer's outfit.

The Idea String. I latched on to the first idea that came to mind: cards. That took a couple of seconds.

The Actionable Idea. I suggested she buy several decks of cards and, using a wide tape, such as duct tape, stick the cards to the tape in long bands, and connect the bands such that she could wear the entire collage as a dress or outfit. I also suggested she procure a smooth cap or hat and stick cards and poker chips to it. Thirdly, she could tape cards or chips to the appropriate earrings and complete the look. I have to admit, my ego did enjoy it when she said, "*That's amazing. And that is a brilliant idea!*"

The Application. Sometimes, situations requiring ideas do not require a lot of analysis. Even if they do, the application of random, creative techniques can establish a mood of fun when generating ideas. People tend to loosen up while playing a game. When tensions are relaxed, the intensity of creativity can be unleashed. You can *bet* on it if you play your creative cards right. (*I couldn't resist. It just occurred to me randomly.*)

CHAPTER 10.

A FEW CREATIVE TRUTHS: VOLUME 3

A brief preamble. This volume of Creative Truths borrows from other creative minds.

1. *"Have no fear of perfection. You'll never reach it."*

Salvador Dali was a Spanish surrealist painter of the 20th century whose work was famous for its symbolism. For many of us, it was simply weird stuff, but the kind of weird that mesmerized. He made no apology for his style or behavior, both of which were as quirky as his creativity on canvas. I used to own a signed reproduction of one of his pieces. I never tired of it, and always saw something different. It reminded me that there is so much to explore in what already exists.

2. *"Creativity requires the courage to let go of certainties."*

Erich Fromm was a German social psychologist of the

20th century. I remember reading his book, "Escape From Freedom," in college. It examines the vulnerabilities inherent in what we think is freedom in our society. His thinking is as relevant today as it was in 1941. It is a challenge to understand that freedom is more of a concept than it is a reality. That, in and of itself, is quite creative.

3. *"The worst enemy to creativity is self-doubt."*

Sylvia Plath was an American writer of poems, novels and short stories. Much of her work was gloomy, to say the least. Not surprisingly, she committed suicide in 1963. It seems that she succumbed to the worst enemy of creativity. She decreated herself.

4. *"Creativity itself doesn't care at all about results—the only thing it craves is the process. Learn to love the process and let whatever happens next happen, without fussing too much about it."*

If you have seen the film, "Eat, Pray, Love," then you have connected to the creativity of American writer, Elizabeth Gilbert, on whose book the film was based. I walked away from this visceral film realizing that I have the opportunity in life to keep discovering things about myself. I would rather keep discovering who I am than simply knowing who I am. Children understand this without knowing that they do. And that's the point.

5. *"Creativity is more than just being different. Anybody can plan weird; that's easy. What's hard is to be as simple as Bach. Making the simple, awesomely simple, that's creativity."*

Charles Mingus, an American jazz bassist, was known as the "Angry Man of Jazz." When sclerosis robbed him of his ability to play in the mid seventies, he continued to compose music until his death in 1979. Anger fueled his process. He was known for chastising audiences clinking glasses during performances and intimidating musical colleagues during recording sessions.

The fact that he was awarded the Grammy Lifetime Achievement Award posthumously in 1997 would probably have made him angry. As a young writer, I was often angry. Anger can fuel creativity, but it kills relationships. When I began to realize that life was easier than I made it out to be, I mellowed. Finding ideas is not a process riddled with complexity. If anything, our creativity allows us, much more easily, to explore the complexity within the simplicity of things

6. *"Creativity comes from looking for the unexpected and stepping outside your own experience."*

Masaru Ibuka is not a household name. But the company this Japanese industrialist co-founded, Sony, is still a juggernaut of technology in the world. What I find most interesting about him is that he believed the most significant human learning occurs within the first three years of life, a proposition discussed in his book, "Kindergarten is Too Late."

I hold to the belief that we keep learning and, more specifically, that we can learn significantly when we open up the scope of our creativity. My own experience with ideation has opened up my intellect and imagination, delivering those ah-hah moments, which are always unexpected.

7. *"Creative thinking—in terms of idea creativity—is not a mystical talent. It is a skill that can be practised and nurtured."*

We welcome back Edward de Bono, the Maltese author and physician who was cited earlier. Besides his writing about lateral thinking, he also produced a documentary, "2040: Possibilities by Edward de Bono." It has no plot or character. In this rather odd production, the viewer never sees Edward; just a sheet of paper on which he draws figures with coloured felt pens. He covers 35 concepts about the future in 90 minutes, with topics ranging from crime and education to the importance of creativity in the workplace.

I have watched YouTube videos featuring him, but unfortunately, there are no excerpts from 2040. However, you might appreciate a video in which he discusses creative thinking using coloured felt pens to illustrate his points. His sense of humour is quite engaging.

http://www.youtube.com/watch

8. *"Our senses are indeed our doors and windows on this*

world, in a very real sense the key to the unlocking of meaning and the wellspring of creativity."

American author Jean Houston is known for her involvement with the Human Potential Movement, the DNA of which can be traced back to the counterculture of the 60s. Houston, whose family tree includes Sam Houston of Texas, assisted Hillary Clinton in the writing of her book, "It Takes a Village," which was authored during her hubby's years in the White House.

When Houston was working on a research project in the early 60s to understand the effects of the drug, LSD, I was learning how to play guitar and marvelling at the Beatles with my sister. It would take another ten years before I experienced the effects of LSD, which happened only once and was, as a gratuitous indulgence in self-exploration, a door and a window to a sleepless night, the details of which my brain and senses don't remember for the most part.

9. *"The role of a creative leader is not to have all the ideas; it's to create a culture where everyone can have ideas and feel that they're valued."*

English Educationalist, Ken Robinson, believed that education should fuel curiosity through creative thinking. I couldn't agree more. When you create a culture within your family or your teams at work wherein ideas are encouraged and valued, productivity increases by leaps and bounds and relationships flourish. In a world crying for innovation, especially in the workplace, this kind of culture galvanizes curiosity and, with certainty (because I have see it happen all the time), invokes the thinking and creativity that lead to Actionable Ideas. Innovation becomes inevitable.

Years ago, I worked with Adrienne and Patrick Duffy (not the actor) and their company, Big Futures, co-scripting and hosting a transformentary film entitled, "Above and Beyond: Exploring the Power of Inspiration in Action." Within the various messages and insights was a focus on "*curiosity in generating new vision and innovation.*" We are naturally curious. To which Adrienne adds, "*Curiosity is an entry point to looking at possibility in your life.*"

The creative process unlocks the door and leads to ideas waiting to be found on the other side. We are always curious, but we don't always act on it. The fact that you are reading this is a good sign that your curiosity is active. You are exploring your creativity and you are considering your own possibilities and dreams. I invite you to find out more about "Above and Beyond" by visiting this link.

www.moonproject.ca

10. *"We choose to go to the moon in this decade and do the other things, not because they are easy, but because they are hard, because that goal will serve to organize and measure the best of our energies and skills, because that challenge is one that we are willing to accept, one we are unwilling to postpone, and one which we intend to win, and the others, too."*

Those words, spoken by American President John F. Kennedy at Rice University in 1962, motivated a half a million people to realize that very lofty goal before the end of the decade. He first stated the goal to Congress on May 25, 1961: *"This nation should commit itself to achieving the goal, before the decade is out, of landing a man on the moon and returning him safely to the earth."*

It also inspired the prequel film to "Above and Beyond" (Creative Truth #9), entitled "The Moon Project," another transformentary film, which I also co scripted and hosted It explores the *"the power of individual leadership and teamwork inspired by great ideas and great passions in a great community."*

Kennedy's idea sits in good company with Pythagoras's proposition that the earth was round and Galileo's theory that the Earth revolved around the Sun. The scientists, engineers, and physicists of the 60s accepted the idea enough to ignore their own ignorance and trust in absolute human potential. Kennedy had engaged collective curiosity. Impossibility transformed itself into the actionable possibility.

What is your "Moon Project"? What is something you dream about that you usually dismiss as impossible? Give it some thought. This is your opportunity to transform "impossible" into "I'm possible." In the meantime, to learn more about Big Futures Moon Project package, which includes the transformentary film, link yourself to it here.

www.moonproject.ca

PART 5.

CHAPTER 11.

CASE STUDIES

I have drawn these cases from a diversity of experience: submissions from people around the world looking for various ideas, advertising campaigns and promotions, strategic creative communication projects, Brilliant Idea workshops, and live events and shows. Some of these Case Studies may not seem relevant to your objective, but even if you have something specific in mind, I still encourage you to read them all. Besides the application of IVLs, there may be other intrinsic values, which can contribute to your thinking and your ideation process. Everyone's creative path is different and unique. There is no absolute recipe. Please bear this in mind when reading the Case Studies.

Each Case Study outlines the steps, beginning with the Context followed by the Idea Strings. The Actionable Idea is clearly described followed by the result, which is the action I took to execute the idea. It will become clear that the idea generation process relies on analysis of the existing circumstances and POVs, which sometimes includes speculation concerning what is not known. Hunches and instincts are influencing factors and unpredictable. The route you take to find an idea for a similar case would probably look very different from mine. There would be similarities, too. In the end, there is no right or wrong way to find an idea.

Each of these Case Studies was seeded within environments affected by various POVs and circumstances. In some cases, the Actionable Ideas were negotiated, because opinions vary, especially when options are involved. With the exception of negative opinions, which may invalidate the process and undermine the motivation of the people in a group, open consideration of ideas guarantees results. I also invite you to send me your favorite Case Study. If it was inspired by a Case Study in this book, explain the connection.

CASE STUDY #1: *THE PINK OF HEARTS*

An art director working for a restaurant in Nambia on the African west coast (the country west of Botswana) needed ideas for a Valentine's dinner event. The colour theme was pink. This was a rich opportunity to use two Inherent Values, **By Implication**, and **Proximity Influence** to get the creativity going.

Events based on special days such as Valentine's are

always fun and trigger ideas immediately, especially because they have so many images, symbols and language already associated with them. This case study applies well to any calendar date special event for a person or organization: theme parties, birthdays, anniversaries, office parties, retirement parties, even product launches, annual general meetings and networking events. The POV can be taken either from the event itself or the person for whom the event is being created.

Step 1. The Context. List the things implied by Valentines and associated with restaurants.

- The colour pink (already a given)
- Hearts, including the traditional heart image
- Love and romance
- Menus (which also implies all printed material such as cards and posters)

Step 2. The Idea String. Identify connections and combinations between the elements.

- Pink and—hearts, romance, menus
- Hearts and—romance, menus (and cards, posters)
- Romance and menus

Step 3. The Actionable Idea. I eventually made the connection between hearts and cards, which suggested a deck of cards, specifically the suit of hearts. I knew that the cards could be used creatively as part of the event, but I still didn't have a theme. So, I played with language and phrases that included the word 'pink,' which either already existed within a common phrase (a colloquialism) or could be used as an alternate for a keyword in a sentence or phrase associated with love and romance as well as phrases or terms associated with playing cards.

- Tickled pink (on Valentines)
- I pink I'm in love
- Pink of me on Valentine's
- The Pink of Hearts

I sent those themes to the art director and here was the result.

They took it one step further.

Summary. The generation of ideas relied primarily on language. Just about everything we do around ideation involves language, which includes words, images and symbols. It is one of the most powerful tools we have.

On a simplistic level, if the name of your organization has a keyword in it, such as "Lion's Business Solutions," all you have to do is search phrases associated with lions to find a theme: "The Lion's Share," "A Roaring Success"—you get the drift. You can even look for language within language, embedded words that lead to ideas.

Let's say you own an art gallery. A search for words and phrases in which the word 'art' is embedded will produce a ready-made Idea String. Using the application on this site, www.scrabblefinder.com/contains/art/, you will find hundreds of words with 'art' imbedded in it. So if you want to set yourself apART, then stART there. It's the smART thing to do.

CASE STUDY #2: *HEAVENLY BEAUTY*

A Singapore packaging company producing a hand-soap called "Heavenly Beauty" needed ideas regarding their packaging. There were two soap products; one made of goat milk for skin whitening and moisturizing, and the other made with papaya known for its exfoliating properties. The existing packaging looked this way:

To generate ideas, I focused first on the Inherent Value, **Function-Result**. First impressions are always valuable.

Step 1. The Context. List the issues relating to the packaging and the product itself.

- The existing packaging evokes "candy bar." The shape and colours of the outer wrap are reminiscent of chocolate bars
- The brand name, "Heavenly Beauty," and the logo are hard in tone, which contradicts the soft nature of the product
- The packaging lacked femininity, a liability given that the target audience was female. There is clearly a disconnect between the function and features of the product and what the packaging is communicating

Step 2: The Idea String. Generate a list focused on shape and colour.

- Knowing the target end user was female, consider the feminine POVs as they relate to personal care products
- Curved, softer shapes: oval, or rounded corners, or, at the very least, emphasize the curved shape or outline if the packaging has to remain square and evoke a sense of natural softness
- Pastel colours also enhance perceptions of softness and purity: off-white or cream, light blue, lavender, but not green or yellow, which in that part of the world are associated with cleaning products

Step 3: The Actionable Idea. The proposed Actionable Idea comprised a list of recommendations. The use of white goats rather than brown goats would accent innocence and purity; however, I suggested that soft-focused images of a woman (photos or illustrations) in a self reflective pose, minimally revealing skin (face, shoulders, arms), would be preferable.

Instead of sliced papaya plants, which resemble vaginas, the plants should be featured whole. An image of a stylized, single drop of milk or papaya juice would illustrate the main ingredient; this could be an element that might be embossed to create a 3-dimensional effect adding depth to the packaging. The use of clouds and light rays would establish a subdued, "heavenly" context. Images of angels would be perceived in a specific religious context and not universal, therefore, not suitable.

Lastly, softer fonts should be employed such as *Italic* (the text style) and more emphasis should be placed on "Heavenly Beauty" rather than "Goatmilk."

The company applied the curves to the actual product, but did not follow through with the outer packaging, with the exception of introducing a curved rainbow and a little more texture in the blue sky. They elected to keep the brown goats.

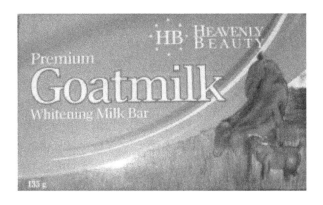

Summary. A physical product is defined by its function and the result it produces. Beyond that, the appeal of that product depends on how it is presented. The Idea String in this case draws upon the product's attributes and how they affect the user. The most critical aspect of creating interest in any physical product is to understand how it appeals to the user from the user's POV. A soap that comes across like a candy bar makes for a weak and confusing brand.

CASE STUDY #3: *THE POLITICIAN'S DILEMMA*

In a small northern town, a young councillor decided to make a bid for the mayor's office. If he won, he would be one of the youngest mayors in the nation. During the campaign, a potentially threatening issue emerged. One of the other candidates uncovered information that the candidate owed back taxes. The amount was not significant, but it was the kind of information the media would exploit in its coverage of the various campaigns.

This was a problem requiring a solution, which meant applying the **Problem-Solution IVL** and **The Other Alternative IVL**. Of course, everyone in the candidate's camp was asking the same question, *"What are we going to do when this goes public?"* We knew it was inevitable; this sensitive information would be exposed. Crisis management begs cooler minds. For me, a problem is always an opportunity, so rather than panic, I looked for the upside in the situation. My search began inside the issues.

Step 1. The Context. Generate a list of issues relating to the problem.

- The information was accurate and true: there were unpaid, outstanding taxes

- The opposing candidate will share the information very quickly with the media; there is little that can be said, which would undo the negativity once the information became known

- The media will pursue the story without hesitation

- The information, if left unaddressed, will cast a disparaging light on the candidate's integrity; his position will be viewed as defensive, further weakening public perception of him as a reliable leader

- The public will judge him quickly; key corporate supporters will distance themselves

Step 2. The Idea String. Determine if there are any possible, immediate solutions. Examine alternative views of the issues and restate them from the point of view of opportunity.

- Pay the outstanding taxes
- Address the information head on; acknowledge the truth; admit that there are unpaid taxes and take responsibility without excuses
- Go on the offensive and face the media when they come calling

Step 3. The Actionable Idea. Having determined that the taxes should be paid immediately, the Idea String led me to pay-dirt. I recommended that he not only pay his taxes, but also *pre-pay* taxes on the current fiscal year. The *pre-payment* was the Actionable Idea.

I advised the candidate to say to the press, in answer to the imminent question about the taxes, *"My taxes are paid. In fact, I have a credit in my tax account, which puts me ahead of the game. And that's where our city will be when I'm Mayor."*

A day or so later, the press came calling. The candidate followed through with the statement and, subsequently, the issue—the problem—faded away and he went on to win the election.

Summary. Often, we look at a problem backwards and get stuck in a negative, single-minded view of it. By examining the issues, eliminating the issues we cannot control, and generating alternative views of the ones we can control within the context of opportunity, we find ideas that have the potential to trigger solutions. When we ignore the negative and emphasize the positive, we can subdue the opposing forces that seek to exploit our vulnerabilities.

CASE STUDY #4: *CAUGHT ON CAMERA*

A large company known as a global workforce accommodation specialist (work camps) was looking for ways to improve their safety training program. With the legislation of stricter safety laws, which hold individuals, not just corporations, accountable for workplace injuries and fatalities, companies were scrambling to improve their safety programs to meet the compliance standards set by the government. The company contracted me to create a video specifically designed to work with their online training resources. The key objective, besides fulfilling the compliance agenda, was to enhance retention.

The challenge was that most of their employees were less educated and did not perform well when it came to reading and understanding the training material, let alone remembering any of it. They needed ideas to be applied to the tone and manner in which the information was to be communicated. Safety is very much about cause and effect, so I focused on the objective using the **Cause-Effect IVL** to find a visual concept and storyline that would fit the bill. It would also require the application of the **Attitude-Altitude IVL** because a shift in their attitude toward safety had to be part of the solution.

Step 1. The Context. List causes and effects associated with safety as well as issues, user behaviors and attitudes associated with safety training.

- Accidents cause injuries, loss of life or livelihood, downtime, lost revenue, higher costs of operating, and physical, emotional and legal turmoil
- Workplace safety incidents affect a company's reputation and expose executives, directors, managers and supervisors to legal liabilities
- Employees are less educated and not comfortable with instructional training
- Employees generally don't enjoy safety training; they see it as something they are obligated to do
- Employees don't take ownership of the safety program and often ignore or disrespect it
- They watch television and surf the net gravitating to programs such as sports, movies and reality shows
- They play video games

Step 2. The Idea String. List the kind of visual media to which employees gravitate. Look for potential connections between their media use and the story telling styles that would be effective in communicating the safety program.

- Popular web videos capture extreme experiences in reality (like accidents, fails and visual gags), and are usually short, attracting high viewership, motivating sharing within the community of peers; they are highly memorable
- Reality shows are generally replete with conflict
- Reality shows are voyeuristic, which implies a hidden camera point of view
- Safety is about reality and can involve conflict
- Hidden cameras include security cameras

Step 3. The Actionable Idea. The connections between reality programming, conflict, and hidden cameras were a recipe for rich, visual stimulation leading to retention. I proposed that we film a series of role-plays involving supervisors and employees, placing them in situations involving accidents, conflicts and abuse between employees—a menu derived from the most common situations inherent in the safety program.

These scenes and mini dramas would be filmed and edited as if they were captured by security cameras throughout the camps. In other words, we would create our own version of a reality show, interlaced with the safety messages and information the company wanted the employees to learn.

The final product was compelling. The results were above expectations. Employees were more engaged and retained a much higher level of the material. An interesting by-product and side effect was that many employees now had the perception that there were security cameras all over the sites, influencing their behavior and attitudes around compliance and safety.

Summary. The success of the final concept was predicated on a strategic understanding of the employee's POV around safety and the nature of their relationship with video media. This case study underscores the value of examining the audience's POV (and attitudes) to trigger ideas leading to a concept that is both relevant and effective.

CASE STUDY #5: *THE PAINT BRUSH*

A young entrepreneur who owned a small house-painting company was struggling with the competition he faced from larger, more established companies. A lack of budget severely limited his ability to advertise on a scale that would generate activity. Sometimes, being a smaller player in a big field can have its advantages. Bigger companies can be slow to react and, as a result, pay less attention to details. These bigger fish are slaves to the systems and processes they created, which makes it harder for them to switch gears and respond to market shifts and changes. Because painting is a service, I started with the **Function-Result** IVL.

Step 1. The Context. List basic aspects relating to house painting including the home owner's POVs relating to house painting.

- Painters use brushes, paint, scaffolds and ladders
- Painters work outside and inside
- Many painters advertise door to door
- Painters identify potential customers by assessing the condition of the home's exterior
- Home owners prefer to do their own painting to save money
- Home owners tend to procrastinate when it comes to making a decision to paint the house (inside or outside)
- When contracting a paint company, home owners will search around for the best price
- Home owners will consult their friends to get references about painters or paint companies they have used

- Home owners are concerned about choosing the right colour and the right paint

Step 2. The Idea String. List the things home owners think about house painting (and other major chores).

- They want someone else to do the job
- They prefer to spend time on more interesting activities when they are home
- They trust that a reputable, professional painter will use the right materials, choose the most suitable colour and do a better job
- Home-owners like getting free offers

Step 3. The Actionable Idea. I didn't have to go too far to make a connection between the basic aspects of house painting and the home-owner's POVs about house painting to establish the Actionable Idea. It led to a simple door to door promotion concept.

I suggested he buy as many inexpensive paint brushes as he could afford and target a neighbourhood where most of the houses showed evidence of needing a paint job. To each paint brush, a note was to be attached and left at the front door of each home. The message on the note was to say, *"Either you can use this free paint brush to do your own painting, or you can call me and I'll do the painting for you while you sit back and have a beer."* I also suggested he offer special package pricing on his services for a limited time.

Summary. Whereas the attributes of the product or service can be easily defined, it is the degree to which we understand the consumer's POVs about benefits of the product or service that helps us find the Actionable Idea.

CASE STUDY #6: MALL OF AMERICA—BATTLE OF BROTHERS

In 1999, the Ghermezian brothers (Triple Five), the creators of West Edmonton Mall and the visionaries and one of the stakeholders in the Mall of America (MOA), the world's largest mall, filed a lawsuit against a co-MOA stakeholder, the Simon Property Group, after the Teachers Insurance and Annuity Association sold half of its 55-percent share in the Mall to the Simon family without informing the Ghermezian brothers. The Ghermezian Brothers took the Simon Brothers to court alleging that the Simons had committed a fiduciary breach. In other words, they violated the partnership agreement.

The defendants, including the Simon Brothers, pointed to a clause in the partnership agreement providing that *"no partner shall be liable to any other partner except in the case of fraud or gross negligence."* In layman's terms, they were implying that Triple Five didn't know what they were doing when it came to the operations and management of the project.

This was where Triple Five brought me in. The objective was to challenge the notion of negligence and assert Triple Five's professionalism, integrity and capabilities in terms of an operation the size of the Mall of America. The guidelines of the court were such that I was limited to a visual presentation without the benefit of including recorded audio. Millions, in fact, billions of dollars were at stake.

Off the starting line, this would require an approach leaning on implications and, by inference, the **By Implication** IVL as well as the other Intuitive IVLs, **Negative Space Thinking** and the **Other Alternative**. It also called for associations through a modified approach using the **Proximity Influence IVL**.

Step 1a. The Context—Part 1. List the images relating to capabilities, professionalism, integrity and credibility as they apply to Triple Five and West Edmonton Mall (WEM). Place an emphasis on images that show largesse and complexity, both visible and not visible to the public

- Aerial views of the WEM and the three phases
- Crowds of shoppers
- Mall decor
- World Waterpark, Amusement Park, the Santa Maria Ship, Skating rink, Mini-golf
- Boilers and power systems in the bowels of the mall

- Water tanks and water systems connected to the Waterpark and the Marine

- Exterior power grid

- Customer information services including security

- Management meeting with visual support such as photos projected on screens, floor plans and schematics

- Signs with symbols or language defining locations, functions and services

- Newspaper clippings relating to the WEM

- Television news clips about WEM showing the broadcaster's brand

- Celebrities appearing at WEM

Step 1b. The Context—Part 2. List issues associated with a presentation that does not include a recorded narrative.

- There is little or no reinforcement of key messages

- Potential confusion may result owing to a lack of clear context, relying only on the viewer to figure out or intuit the meaning of the sequences and individual images

- It is difficult to establish an emotional connection to the story

Step 2. The Idea String. List story concepts and presentation style options.

- Silent movies can be compelling as long as the plot line is clearly established from the beginning; a silent documentary capturing the size and scope of WEM can be easily supported through the impressive, large scale visuals, as well as the diversity of operations

- Very few people see the behind-the-scenes operations and equipment, which represents a visual opportunity to present the complexities inherent in operating a building of WEM's magnitude; it also introduces the viewer to the sizable team responsible for WEM's operations

- The existing archive of media coverage surrounding the ongoing story and evolution of WEM supports the credibility of the team responsible for its creation, development and operations; it exemplifies and proves consistency and forward thinking

- There is no other story comparable to WEM except for that of the Mall of America; subsequently, the similarities between the two giant monoliths implies a highly relevant and important connection, which validates the Ghermezian's involvement

Step 3. The Actionable Idea. It was determined by the lawyers that someone could speak to the images in court, but this would require a significant amount of rehearsal and depend on the skill of the live narrator. But, how much narrative would work without becoming disjointed or out of step with the video? It was risky and, at one point, we debated whether it should be a slide show. My sense was that static images would weaken the impact of what we were trying to communicate. It would look and feel less sophisticated, which impacts credibility.

There was certainly enough content available to capture. It was more a question of the sequencing and how we associated the images and, even though there would be a limited narrative, there would be much in the way of missed messaging that we would have to make up for with visuals as our only vehicle.

I returned to my Father's philosophy that to visualize the building you have to understand the land first. This led me to the design of the video I felt would achieve the objective. In this case, I reversed my Father's strategy and decided to show the obvious first and then reveal the complexity therein. In some ways, I owed my Father for this Actionable Idea.

Each section of the story would be aligned with each phase of the mall. We would digitally highlight each phase using an aerial view of the mall. We would take the viewer into each phase and start with the key highlights, relying on signage (language implied visually) to articulate location wherever it was available.

Then we would go below the deck to the bowels of the mall to reveal the systems and equipment supporting the operation of each phase. Because some of the bigger, more complex mall attractions are in the third phase, the visual story would grow in scope, finishing with the massive underwater technologies supporting the large Water Park.

The animated, management meeting in the filled boardroom included well timed close-ups of the schematics of the electrical power grid. The associated text on the schematics clarified the context.

By associating the major systems with their respective areas of application (proximity), the sequences told a story about organization, structure, and planning on a large scale, which implies expertise and professionalism.

The video was a lesson in how *less* can be *more.* The result? The court found that there was nothing in the Simon Brothers argument that proved "fraud or gross negligence" on the part of their partner, Triple Five, rendering the issue moot and dispelling the only potential threat to the Ghermezian's case.

In September, 2003, The Triple Five Group won its lawsuit against Simon Properties. The Ghermezian brothers were awarded half the Mall's profits from the previous four years and they were allowed the opportunity to buy 27.5 percent of the Mall of America from the Simon family, raising them to majority stakeholder and managing partner. The Ghermezians now own the Mall of America outright and it continues to thrive.

The letter I received from Nader Ghermezian acknowledged the critical role the silent video played in their litigation.

Summary. Silence is negative space. It provides us with an opportunity to focus the lens in a way that can make images and messaging more powerful. It forces us to look for language and meaning inside the images, from the blatant signs to the magnificent, physical displays and structures, the products and evidence of our capabilities as visionaries, builders and creators. The implications are always amazing.

CASE STUDY #7: *JESUS AND THE LEPERS*

My original career plan was to become a stage actor. As a young man, I had the opportunity to study acting with veteran Canadian thespian, Douglas Rain, best known for his performance as the voice of Hal, the computer, in Stanley Kubrick's iconic science fiction film, *2001, A Space Odyssey*.

Rewind. The one thing I remember, which has stayed with me to this very day, is a creative point he made about performance in one of his classes. The focus of the class was on establishing character the first time an actor appears on the stage. He then proceeded to walk on *backwards* and then whipped around and launched into a monologue. It was an inspiring moment and became the DNA of my understanding of what I call "the reveal." Rain did the unexpected and it was incredibly memorable.

Fast Forward. As the director of a large-scale, amateur production of "Jesus Christ Superstar," I was wrangling up to 60 performers. The transitions between scenes were complicated, especially because, at the time, there were no wireless microphones. (Just in case you didn't know, Superstar is a rock musical.) It was a spaghetti twist of cables on the stage, and the blocking logistics (meaning how actors move on the stage) were nothing short of organized chaos.

In the Temple scene, Jesus destroys the stalls and forces the money changers and prostitutes to leave. Jesus wanders alone outside the city, but is confronted by a crowd of lepers, all wanting to be healed, overwhelming him with their pleas for help.

The directorial challenge was to stage the transition from the chaos of the temple to the subsequent chaos with the lepers, minimizing the complexity of transferring several microphones from one group of actors to another. (Even if we would have had wireless microphones, the challenge would have been similar.) The solution involved the application of the **Negative Space IVL**.

Step 1. The Context. List the elements and issues relating to the physical situation for both scenes.

- Both scenes feature many actors
- Space is limited, owing to the number of money changer tables, several boxes and bags on several stage levels
- Dozens of microphones need to change hands
- The music is seamless, not allowing for a lot of time for a smooth transition

Step 2. The Idea String. List the transition options and assess their viabilities.

- In the dark, have the temple actors exit and the leper actors enter and take their stage positions, exchanging microphones; exchanging microphones quickly in the dark is problematic or, at the very least, time consuming

- Include the lepers with the temple actors in the temple scene and have the temple actors hand the microphones to the lepers during the transition; although it swells the crowd numbers, it is weak creatively because the lepers are not in the temple from the story point of view and to disguise them creates a costume change issue during a transition

- Hide the lepers behind the higher, rear stage at the beginning of the temple scene and, while the temple actors exit, the lepers can take their position; this makes the microphone exchange difficult, although alternatively, the microphones can be left on the stage; however, that forces the lepers to find the microphones in the dark

- Have the lepers walk on at the beginning of the leper scene with the stage lit as Jesus sings, either from off stage, or from hidden positions on the stage and pick up their microphones; there's no problem with the solution, but it is quite basic and traditional and lacks mystery; it also looks clunky when they have to pick up their microphones

Step 3. The Actionable Idea. The Actionable Idea I liked was to hide the lepers on stage or behind the stage so that they would be revealed (taking a page from Douglas Rain). Even though I still did not have a clear, creative solution, my instinct told me that the answer was somewhere within, so I kept looking.

I re-examined the elements, objects and structures on the stage. A thought occurred to. What if their costumes were such that they could look like tattered bags? The problem was that they would still have to take their positions just as the temple scene began and the audience might catch them in the act. The Actionable Idea I needed was to hide them in plain sight. Finally, a derivative of this idea occurred to me. Put the lepers *in* the bags.

I had set and prop people create sturdy, sizable bags that could be easily dragged onto the stage at the beginning of the temple scene. The temple actors would drag the bags on with the lepers in them. Some of the actors were actually able to carry their bags over their shoulders for the actors inside who were light weight and smaller.

At the end of the temple scene, the temple actors left the microphones very close to the bags, which were, of course, also left on the stage. I had the lighting designer set the lights for a dusky look, somewhat dim with subtle highlights. As Jesus transitioned into the leper scene, the bags began to stir and move. The lepers eventually emerged. Other lepers joined the crowd from hidden positions behind the stage to swell the ranks. At the moment the lepers began to emerge from the bags, the audience let out a collectively amazed "ooooooo."

The proximity of the microphones made it easy for the actors to grab them as they crawled out of the bags and to their feet. The transition was completely seamless and remarkable, especially because we never had to completely dim the stage. Thank you, Mr. Rain.

Summary. Sometimes, the best place to hide something is in plain sight; classic, negative space thinking. What is also important is to recognize when you have a hunch based on other Actionable Ideas. If you feel you may have missed something, you're probably right. That's your opportunity to go back and re-examine the elements and issues you have already listed. When you have a team around you contributing to the analysis, the Actionable Idea will be found.

CASE STUDY #8: *THE SURPRISE SYMPHONY*

Since directing Superstar, I have always looked for the chance to apply "the reveal" whenever I am staging an event or show. On one occasion, I was directing a large corporate event for the local Chamber of Commerce. The local Youth Symphony Orchestra was invited to perform and, given the staging set-up, we faced a challenge. How would we transition into their performance without encumbering the process and the audience's experience? Also, I was a stickler for seamless shows and still have an aversion for shows filled with gaps, such as when speakers are introduced and take a long walk to the podium after their name is called. Pregnant, endless pauses. Never on my watch.

There were over 20 young musicians with their instruments and the main stage was already pre-set for the major feature performance that evening. Space was at a premium. A second stage was a possibility, but I didn't want the transition to become noisy and awkward. The other element involved was a pre-produced video telling their story, which was to play just before their performance.

With the Superstar experience in my back pocket, I latched onto the **Negative Space Thinking IVL** to find the Actionable Idea.

Step 1. The Context. List the elements and issues relating to the physical situation in which the transition to the youth orchestra performance occurs.

- The orchestra will be assembled back stage with their instruments
- The sound gear to be used on stage will be pre-set
- A short video will play before their performance
- The audience does not know they will perform

Step 2. The Idea String. List the staging options and related issues.

- Set up a second stage; if the stage is rolled in, it will cause a distraction; if the stage is not preset, the set-up will also cause a distraction
- Pre-set a second stage behind the audience and

disguise it with curtains, and lighting effects so it was not too obvious; there will still be noise when the musicians take their positions

- Don't use a stage; set-up the orchestra on the floor; visibility will be poor even with live cameras covering the performance

Step 3. The Actionable Idea. The Actionable Idea emerged when I connected the video and the disguised, pre-set stage. It was convenient that I was producing the video to be played before the performance, because I could ensure that it kept the audience's attention, both their eyes and ears, on the screens located on either side of the main stage. The one thing left to do was establish the logistics that would minimize the time it would take and the noise the musicians would make when they took their positions. The video would play a large role in masking this activity.

Before an orchestra performs, they play what is simply called a "tuning" or "orchestra tuning." The oboe player starts it off by playing the "A" note and, then, the sections join in pursuant to the conductor's cue, playing the same "A" note. I had the orchestra perform this ritual for the video and directed the editor of the video to make sure it was as loud as it could be without distorting during playback.

The orchestra was assembled backstage in a very specific order to make sure they could all get to their seats in under 2 minutes, which they would do when the video started playing. Once seated, they would wait to hear the "tuning" in the video. When the tuning started to play, they slowly joined in (still hidden behind the curtain), syncing up to the video audio track.

They were instructed to start softly (to creep into the sound mix as it were) and get louder until the curtain to their stage was opened. As the live tuning began to swell, the sound mixer slowly faded the audio level of the video. The video director had the switcher transition from the video to the live cameras on the orchestra as the curtain opened. The lights on the stage were completely dimmed as the lights on the second stage at the rear of the audience were brought up.

The effect was stunning and the audience fell into a collective "oooooo" as their heads and bodies turned to the source of the new, live sound. It was a moment of realization coupled with a physical experience. The sound of the orchestra travelled from the front of the room (video) to the back (live orchestra) in a stereo wave. Voila! A surprise symphony.

Summary. The execution of an event, whether it occurs in a small, break-out room at a conference or in a substantial performance venue, is enhanced with the use of multi-media. There is always an opportunity to explore the options that can be generated when using pre-recorded elements with live elements. The key is to list those options and seek out the connections between all the assets being deployed. The ideas lurk within waiting to be exposed and applied.

The by-product of an Actionable Idea is its application in other circumstances. I have used "the reveal" in several live situations and also applied the concept in video production and even script writing. Once an Actionable Idea has been executed, the learnings derived fuel future

Idea Strings. Knowledge is cumulative; innovation breeds innovation. Cross pollination is always possible.

CASE STUDY #9: *FOUR STRONG WINDS*

The Winspear Centre in Edmonton is a world class performance venue. Some of the most renowned artists in the world have performed there. It was my privilege to be asked to write, produce and direct the Prairie Music Awards (now the Western Canadian Music Awards), which would involve many live performances as well as a tribute to a Canadian musical icon, Ian Tyson. The show would also be aired live on CBC Radio. The promoters gave me the creative license to have fun. As long as the awards were presented and CBC received the number of requisite, live IDs (identifications or "brought to you by" announcements), I had the freedom to use humour and multi-media to enhance the entertainment value.

I knew the approach would involve an alternative way of producing an award show, so that the evening would not become dulled by nominee reels and acceptance speeches. Given the number of awards being handed out, the possibility of the event turning into a drone fest was glaring. It meant looking for alternatives using the **Other Alternative IVL**.

Step 1. The context. List the elements and issues relating to the show.

- Numerous awards are to be presented in 2 hours
- Various live acts will perform in different genres
- Ian Tyson will receive a special honour
- The show is being simulcast live on radio
- CBC requires a specified number of IDs (identifications)
- The budget is challenged

Step 2. The Idea String. List possible alternatives in presenting various aspects of the show.

- Use pre-recorded video elements wherever possible, allowing for humour to be injected into the overall presentation
- Consider the use of multiple hosts, rather than one host
- Break up the sections of Ian Tyson's story rather than present it in one component; examine potential, story through-lines based on this thinking and ask the question, *"What can connect the storyline?"*
- Consider alternative ways of fulfilling CBC's request regarding their broadcast IDs

- Examine the musical context to find ideas within songs and styles of performance

Step 3a. The Actionable Idea—CBC Station IDs. *"You're listening to CBC Radio."* Radio networks need their fix and that's why you hear their "ID" several times an hour. It seems obsessive, but that's the way it is. Understanding this, I asked myself, *"How can we make these basic station Ids more interesting?"* The answer to this question was the alternative. What if someone other than CBC voiced their station ID? Then, another alternative came to mind. What if several other people voiced the station ID? And yet, another alternative. What if they made fun of it, subject to CBC's approval?

The Other Alternative occurred to me when I chased the idea of filming the alternative IDs. What if various other people performed humorous, perhaps even ridiculous station Ids on camera and they were used as interstitials? (Interstitials are short elements filling the gap between two other major events.) CBC approved, subject to a final review.

With that conditional nod, I sent out requests to various artists who would be appearing at the show to come up with their own version of a CBC ID, providing that somewhere in their script, they said, *"You're listening to the Prairie Music Awards live on CBC Radio 2."* They could sing it, do it as a skit, look confused, or be notorious, just as long as there were no expletive deletives (profanities) and they were not slanderous or offensive to gender or culture.

The artists jumped at the opportunity and the end-result was hilarious. In addition, I didn't have too much work to do. CBC loved them and, in fact, told me after the show that their booth announcer never had to say a thing during the show, because we had covered off the requirement and then some.

Step 3b. The Actionable Idea—Honouring Ian Tyson. I wanted to avoid the predictably predictable. (yes, I'm being redundantly redundant.) I expected that just about every artist appearing in the show, as well as the artists winning awards, would want to say something about Ian Tyson. I knew it was inevitable. This was the key to the Actionable Idea. I wondered if there was another way we could pay homage to this musical icon and do it with style and even a little, respectable humour.

Some of the alternatives were already exhausted. I didn't want to duplicate what we were doing with the CBC IDs, so I turned my attention to Ian's story and his music. The Idea String had already established two ideas: break up the story; examine songs and styles of music.

At first, I thought it might be interesting to have the selected artists performing at the show to revamp a portion of one of their songs to include something about Ian's story; however, I reminded myself that these artists are very busy, and given the timelines, it might be too time consuming for them. The Other Alternative was inherent in that idea. All it required was simplification.

I asked each of the artists if they would perform a few bars of "Four Strong Winds," a hit song Ian wrote in the early 60s and performed with his then partner, Sylvia (Ian & Sylvia). It was one of the most popular songs of the folk revival era. The twist I added was that they perform the excerpt in their own style, whether it was traditional or contemporary country, rock, rap, rockabilly—whatever the genre. I even asked a group called Fubuki Daiko, a Japanese drum group, to craft their own version, notwithstanding the fact that their musical style made it very challenging to interpret Ian's classic hit. The musicians didn't need much convincing.

On the night of the show, the audience, including Ian Tyson, enjoyed several weird and wonderful versions of a song that has been played on radio for decades. When Ian Tyson accepted his honour that night, he opened his speech by saying, *"I think my favorite version of that song was Fubuki Daiko's."*

Summary. This case study underscores the value of not only generating alternatives, but also connecting them. Look at two alternatives (or more) together. You are not required to know immediately why or even how they might be connected. It is even possible they don't connect, at least, not at first blush. So, in that case, stop thinking about it and let your sub-conscious brain and instinct do the rest. When the mind has done its thing, something will occur to you. In some cases, the connection you make will be, in fact, the Other Alternative and the Actionable Idea.

CASE STUDY #10: *THE PHONE BUTLER*

Creating a product from scratch was one of the most rewarding experiences I have ever had. What I learned from the process has contributed to a more enlightened understanding of marketing.

Some time before digital technology became the norm; people used analog answering machines, which required the user to record an outgoing message using the built-in microphone. There were two tapes in the machines; one, looped, self-cueing tape for the outgoing message and one tape to capture incoming messages from callers. Typical answering machines would automatically add a signal (the infamous beep), which cued the tape that would capture the incoming messages.

Pre-recorded answering messages, many of them comical, were already available in the market, but the method of using them was cumbersome because the user would have to play the message using a second machine, which would be recorded through the microphone of the user's machine. There were no customized, looped tapes that could be loaded directly into an answering machine and work. The problem was the resident signal (the beep). Different machines had different signals.

I also decided to write a book, which I would fill with

scripted answering messages of all types: humorous, basic, and seasonal. This case involved four IVLs: **Function-Result, Problem-Solution, Negative Space Thinking** and **The Other Alternative**. I have simplified the details in each of the steps, because the product development phase had many aspects to it, too many to list in their entirety.

Step 1: The Context. Examine the current market in terms of similar products, and list the design and production challenges for the tapes and the book.

- There are no other answering message publications on the market and there are no books of any kind in phone stores
- Similar cassette tape products do not have a strong branding style
- There are various answering message tapes, but they require a second machine to use
- There are standard packaging configurations for cassette tapes
- How-to books are popular
- The creative answering message is the Unique Selling Proposition and everything should communicate this context

Step 2: The Idea String. Formulate the thinking around the brand and list possible alternatives to deal with the technological limitations. Once again, I have simplified this list. Both the Context and the Idea String are always in flux and evolving throughout the process, especially when creating a product from scratch.

- Develop the overall brand and book titles that are simple and quickly communicate the brand, USP and the content to consumers; research images and symbols relating to phones
- Consider a design for all components that minimizes printing costs with a view to the optimum minimum, possibly one colour (black and white format)
- Determine the size of the book that minimizes paper stock costs and is favourable to retailers from a merchandising point of view, including configurations for impulse-buy merchandise in store racks (the kind one sees at the check-out till)
- Consult with engineers and understand how the cueing signal technology works and determine if there are technical alternatives

Step 3. The Actionable Idea. In this case, there were several Actionable Ideas. Let's start with the overall brand.

I began by researching images of phones: old-fashioned, modern, stylized, graphic and photographic. The issue for me was that the image of the phone on its own did not really invoke the context of the answering message. So, I left the exercise for awhile and let my brain work on connecting the dots. Then, the Actionable Idea emerged.

One night, I was watching an old movie and, in one scene, the butler answers the phone. Need I say more? I connected "phone" and "butler" and began to draw images of a butler answering the phone until I arrived at this high-contrast, stylized logo.

The tuxedo added a touch of class and, additionally, it could all be produced in black and white, the most inexpensive printing option. This funky interpretation of a classical image in a stylized form would be easily applied to every aspect of the product, both the book and the cassette tapes.

Next, I considered the title of the book. The initial list was colourful, but none of the titles seemed to jump out. I wanted to be clear that the book was about "telephone answering messages," but it seemed somewhat pedantic to call it, "Telephone Answering Messages" or "Creative Answering Messages." Frustrated, I began to research titles of how-to books and I noticed that the ones catching my eye and my brain had a number in them.

Then I researched other book titles featuring a number in them, such as Stephen Covey's "The 7 Habits of Highly Effective People" and Ken Blanchard's and Spencer

Johnson's "One Minute Manager." I was intrigued with Covey's use of the numeral form of '7' rather than the word form of it, "seven." I note that he did the same thing with "The 3rd Alternative." (You may begin to notice in this case study the DNA for the title of this book, "A Brilliant Idea Every **60** Seconds.")

From there, I considered the fact that the book would contain dozens of messages, so, I played around with the actual number. Almost immediately, I put the title "100 Answering Messages" on the list. Then I researched expressions and turns of phrase including "100." What emerged were a few colloquialisms using "101" rather than just "100." That was the trigger for "101 Telephone Answering Messages." The book's concept was complete.

Of course, the cassette tapes would not contain 101 recorded messages. But, I had other problems with that product component. I was determined to create a cassette tape that could be loaded directly into an answering machine and become functional immediately, without the user having to mess around with a recording transfer.

The phone company technician I consulted with told me that there were a number of different, resident signals in the answering machines on the market (about a half dozen). It would be impossible to use one particular signal for all of them. That would mean I would have to produce various versions of each cassette tape, a costly and problematic option. Then, an idea occurred to me. (The brain had been working while I wasn't looking.)

I asked the technician if all the standard signals could be recorded onto the same tape, which meant the answering machine would have to identify its own particular signal. At first, the technician said it wasn't possible, but he didn't know for sure. This was a classic case of knowing what we don't know. So I asked him if he would test it out. His opinion was that the presence of other signals playing at the same time might confuse the machine's ability to read the resident signal.

So I provided him with various tapes, one with two different signals, and another with three and so on up to the number of signals known to be in use. He completed the test and advised me that my hunch was right. The various machines responded to their specific signals, including the tape with all the signals. I was able to produce just one tape for all the answering machine brands.

The project went on to great success. Over fifty thousand copies of the book were sold across Canada through the various telephone companies and their retail stores. The number may seem small by American standards, but in Canada, it is quite significant. The number sold earned the book its designation as a National Best Seller.

Thousands of tapes were also sold. I eventually sold my interest in the project to my partner and moved on. To my knowledge, there is no answering message book on the market at this writing. Maybe it's time to produce "1001 Telephone Answering Messages."

Summary. Products (and services) offer at least three starting points for the development of a brand's identity: its function, the manner in which it is used and the result it produces. From there, we can find ideas within associated images and language. In the case of The Phone Butler, the Actionable Idea was inspired almost accidently. This case study offers more evidence of how we can have faith in our brains to do the work and to be receptive to suggestion. Some of the work is already done, which is why we will recognize or find the Actionable Idea when we least expect it.

As for my hunch about the technology? It is an example of remaining loyal to an objective and trusting in instinct. Anything we consider impossible invites us to challenge the notion. There might not be a direct solution, but there are always alternatives. Sometimes, hunches work out. Never underestimate your wildest notions. They are ideas begging attention.

Lastly, the lessons learned carry forward. I now have a thing about numbers. It's embedded in my brain. Not much time goes by when I do not consider values or concepts involving numbers. It still amazes me how much our connection to the world has something to do with a number—everything from money and time to superstitions. Next to those numbers are the ideas you can count on.

CASE STUDY #11: *TRUTH IN ADVERTISING*

Radio is a wonderful medium. From a creative point of view, it forces the copywriter into brevity. As creative professionals working in a medium without visuals, we have to consider how people hear information or interpret dialogue through their ears.

About audiographics. On a website called the "Urban Dictionary," you will find a term I coined in 2008, "audiographic," which is defined as *"a mental image stimulated by sound; an image in the mind generated by an audio sound or effect; picture thoughts; elements of photographic memory; technical term used in audio and radio production. When you hear an audiographic, like glass breaking in a radio commercial, you think and see, in your mind, the image of glass breaking. Your thought is not in word form, but rather in the form of a mental image or an audiographic."*

The other critical factor radio copywriters have to take into account is that the words we write are spoken. There is a significant difference between writing words to be read versus writing words to be spoken and heard. Many corporate presentations fall flat, because the authors write it in a form that might be understood more clearly when it is read, versus when it is spoken.

Beyond ideas, it is critical to understand the medium in which we are expressing those ideas. Slogans, headlines, titles, copy blocks on the web—whatever the form—they are processed through our senses. When we get caught in the vortex of thinking about them only from an intellectual point of view, we fail to express them in a way that will accommodate the POVs of our audience. Those POVs are accessed through a sensory experience with many filters, intellectual and emotional.

When a new dealership came to me for an advertising campaign, the dealer principal, a brilliant young man by the name of Scott Held, told me he wanted to *"tell the truth"* or *"shoot from the hip"* in his advertising.

He had an aversion to promotional gimmicks and aggressive, hard sell radio commercials. His position was that consumers were well informed and savvy enough to see through the fabricated, superficial offers.

My consultation to him at the time was simple; if you're going to tell the truth, then, *tell* the truth. Cheesy won't work. Clever humour can still convey the truth. Satire rich in irony is an intelligent form of communicating issues and contexts.

Over several years, we produced hundreds of commercials. I have selected a few examples with scripts to illustrate how a very simple idea—to tell the truth in advertising—becomes a clear guideline ensuring the continuity of communication and engagement between an advertiser and the targeted consumer.

Many IVLs were used, but overall, this campaign, which has also been applied in television, in print and on the web, included the **By Implication IVL,** the **Proximity Influence IVL** and the **Attitude-Altitude IVL.** When an advertiser stands next to a believable truth, they establish credibility and a meaningful, long term relationship with consumers.

Step 1. The Context. Establish the basic context of truth in advertising. List the substantive demands of what the dealership wants and, truthfully, doesn't want from the consumer. Also list the basic implications the dealership knows about consumers.

- We want them to buy vehicles from us
- We need their business
- We don't *care* about them personally, meaning, we don't look at them as "one of the family"; we see them as informed, intelligent people with money making a significant investment; so, we respect them
- We don't sell cars below cost because we have bills and salaries to pay
- We don't buy into gimmicks, such as giveaways, contests, bonuses, free stuff, endorsements from local sports celebrities who don't really care about the dealership but are happy to drive a free vehicle
- We don't have the lowest prices, which doesn't mean our prices are unreasonable
- We know consumers shop around
- We are not perfect; we make mistakes and do what we can to correct them

Step 2. The Idea String. List the ideas such that they are directly connected to the context elements.

- State the ideas using the language in the contexts; i.e. *we need your business*

- Use the vernacular employing common turns of phrase consumers will quickly understand and believe; i.e. *we have to pay bills*

- Develop situations that reflect the reality of the dealership in doing business in a competitive market; i.e. *we don't sell vehicles below cost because we would go out of business*

- Avoid using complex conditions, such as long, multifaceted disclaimers; i.e. *this offer is limited and conditions apply, see dealer for details, not valid with any other offer*

- Poke fun at the competition to illustrate how the dealership is different in its approach to consumers; expose the other guy's tactics

- Focus on topical, current issues of which consumers are aware, especially when using satire or humour

- If the creative premise of any particular campaign at any time does not feel real or believable, do not pursue it

Step 3. The Actionable Idea. The following scripts tell the story.

Hi, Scott here Sherwood Park Dodge. I suppose that, as a new dealership, we could advertise like many other dealerships do and scream in your ear about big discounts and the lowest prices. But you've heard it all before, so the question I ask myself is this—why not keep it simple? What if I just tell you: we're a new dealership. we need customers, and we have to offer you lower prices. Nothing fancy. Just the plain truth. And that—we hope—is what you will find does make Sherwood Dodge different. (*LOCATION TAG*)

Hi, Scott here from Sherwood Dodge. You know by now we're a new dealership and, of course, we have to advertise if we want to do business. But, we're not all that keen on the promotional hype thing. You know what I mean, like "The owner is out of town and we're slashing prices." Well, I'm the owner and I'm right here 'cause we have work to do. And we're not overstocked, because we actually manage our inventory sensibly. So, we're offering the best price we can because we need customers. (*LOCATION TAG*)

Hi, I'm Scott here from Sherwood Dodge. I realize that a lot of dealerships tell you about friendly knowledgeable staff, the best service, that things are done right the first time. Well, sometimes, we don't do it right the first time because we're human at Sherwood Dodge. BUT—we '*do*' what we have to—to *get* it right because that's what I think is meant by service among other things. And even though we have a friendly knowledgeable staff, we're '*knowledgeable*' enough to know that you're here to buy a vehicle and not socialize. (*LOCATION TAG*)

SCOTT: Hi. Scott here from Sherwood Dodge. You know those hard sell commercials? Let me translate some things for you. Okay, go ahead.

MAK: "Now for a limited time, get our lowest prices."

SCOTT: Which means, *"limited to forever."*

(*TO ANNOUNCER*) Keep going.

MAK: "It's our anniversary and we're celebrating!"

SCOTT: Which means, *"We're running out of themes. But you can expect plenty of balloons."* (*TO ANNOUNCER*) One more for the ditch.

MAK: "If you don't buy now, you could miss the greatest—"

SCOTT: *"Greatest"* what? Means absolutely nothing. How about—

"If you don't buy now, good for you. When you're ready, so are we."

MAK: That's crazy!

SCOTT: (*CASUALLY*) Stop it. (*LOCATION TAG*)

Scott here from Sherwood Dodge. You know those ads that say: "We have to sell 45 vehicles by Friday or we'll spontaneously combust." Well, Sherwood Dodge has to sell 45 vehicles by Friday because, frankly, I'm tired of looking at them. They're the last of the XX models. Cars, trucks, SUV's, with savings up to XX thousand dollars and more, which is depressing for me to say, but good news for you. We're also offering 0 percent financing on most models. So please buy one. We're calling it the year end clearance. Not too creative, but that's what it is. That's this week 'til Friday at Sherwood Dodge, 'cause then I'm auctioning them off to other dealerships. (*LOCATION TAG*)

Scott here for Sherwood Dodge. I'm not going to pussy foot around. June sucked for used sales. So we're having a *"Big Used Vehicle Event Because June Sucked Sale."* We have nearly 50 late model low mileage cars in stock. Like an 07 Caliber SXT, nice options, only XX bucks. We have mini vans from as low as XX. SUVs from XX. Dodge half tons and diesels from XX. All inspected, certified and ready to go.   The *"Big Used Vehicle Event Because June Sucked Sale,"* now at Sherwood Dodge. *(LOCATION TAG)*

Scott here for Sherwood Dodge. You know those ads where they tell you they're selling their vehicles below cost. Well I can't sell vehicles below cost and I don't know how *they* can unless they enjoy committing economic suicide. So, I decided that Sherwood Dodge is going to have the "Above Cost" sale. And some vehicles are just above cost. Cause we need customers and I need to move out some inventory. And I'm not going to insult your intelligence. If the other guys are offering below cost deals, ask for the paperwork to prove it. Sherwood Dodge. *(LOCATION TAG)*

Scott here from Sherwood Dodge. Recently I heard that some people find my commercials annoying. Frankly I find most commercials annoying but I thought I would try to be *less* annoying. So, for the next seconds, sit back and enjoy this special selection from my collection of soothing sounds for people who find me annoying. *(SFX: soothing spa music)* Ok. Kill the music. *(music stops abruptly)* Now for the annoying part. We need your business, so give us a shot. Visit our website and buy a truck or something. *(Off mic)* Was that too annoying?

GORD: So, Scott, you got any advice for all the folks going back to school?

SCOTT: Yah. Stick to the basics, like we do at Sherwood Dodge.

GORD: Sorta like: never drink downstream from your horse.

SCOTT: More like we price our vehicles right, right up front. No gimmicks. No sketchy below cost deals. Sherwood Dodge needs customers and customers want the straight goods.

GORD: Well, your buckle ain't gonna shine in the dirt unless you get up.

SCOTT: That's what makes Sherwood Dodge the number one selling dealer of Ram Trucks in Canada, year after year. Puts Sherwood Dodge in a *class* of its own.

GORD: You were dyin' to say that, weren't you . . .

SCOTT: Scott here from Sherwood Dodge. We tried to get a big name hockey player to be our spokesperson. Truth is, we couldn't afford it. But we did find someone and here he is from the Swedish beer league, Bjorn Jaegerstick.

BJORN: Halla.

SCOTT: So what position do you play?

BJORN: Jag är den utrustning som chef för is hockey. (*I'm the equipment manager for the hockey team.*)

SCOTT: You're the equipment manager.

BJORN: Jag ville spela men jag har ingen talang. (*I wanted to play but I have no talent.*)

SCOTT: You wanted to play but you have no talent.

BJORN: Ja (*Yes.*)

SCOTT: Well that certainly kicks this whole thing up a notch. Sherwood Dodge. Just say Bjorn sent you.

BJORN: Björn skickade till dig.
SCOTT: *You* don't have to say it.

SCOTT: Scott here from Sherwood Dodge. One thing about our salespeople . . . they work hard to do it right, right up front.
GORD: (*a character sounding like "Rocky"*): Salespeople are expendable.
SCOTT: Not really.
GORD: What you need is heavy artillery and all the intel you can get. Go in. No mercy. Get it done. Close the deal.
SCOTT: And this is what you think will work at Sherwood Dodge?
GORD: Smack, pack 'em and rack 'em. Bob's your uncle
SCOTT: I don't have an uncle called Bob.
GORD: This is the car industry. Take no prisoners.
SCOTT: Sherwood Dodge.
GORD: So, do I got a shot or what?
SCOTT: Your chances are a little 'rocky.'
GORD: You kiddin' me?

Summary. For years, Scott's dealership has been one of the top truck selling dealerships the country. He has influenced the automotive market in his market to the point where listeners rarely hear a hard sell commercial from any dealership anymore. Other dealers try to emulate him, but it is clear they do not have a clear strategy. Trying to sound like the other guy does not produce a believable message.

Customers have confirmed in person, on the phone and by email that they appreciate the attitude and philosophy communicated in his advertising. They also confirm that their buying experience with the sales representatives echoes the message they keep hearing. Another aspect of this campaign is that it is sustainable. Telling the truth is the main criteria for creative development. We talk about real things and there are always real things to talk about.

This radio advertising campaign, one of the most successful in my career, reminds me that the implications in a message can have a profound effect on consumers' thinking. An advertiser can prove their brand integrity and value without blatantly saying they have it with such empty statements like, *"At our dealership, the customer is always number one."* When you tell people what you are *really* thinking, the message will get through, *by implication.*

CASE STUDY #12: *AN OLYMPIC IDEA*

The University of Alberta needed a television commercial. They had purchased a healthy package of commercials to air during the 2006 Winter Olympics. The context of the message was encumbered by politics and restrictions, including those of the International Olympic Committee (IOC). On top of that, the timeline to produce the campaign was excruciatingly tight, because it involved an approval process with the Olympic

Committee, the broadcaster and the University's public affairs team.

I was pulled off a filming location in mid-directorial stride and whisked over to the initial meeting where I was met with a herd of public affairs people who were scrambling to get a grip on the creative process. I sat quietly for the first half hour, analyzing the personalities in the room and formulating a creative approach based on the issues being tabled. I roamed through this creative adventure paddling with several IVLs, but I relied primarily on **Negative Space Thinking** and **The Other Alternative**.

Step 1. The Context. List everything falling onto the discussion table paying particular attention to the political issues associated with the message's objective to promote the University.

- The broadcast context is national, which implies an east versus west mentality; the University is concerned with making statements or claims that might raise the ire in other universities, educational organizations and even the public, especially in the east

- The Olympic Committee is concerned about messages around University sports programs being associated with or somehow connected to the Olympic paradigm; I found this somewhat odd, but, then again, I'm used to 'odd'; I interpreted this to mean that the IOC did not want to be construed as an endorser of the University's sports programs

- The visuals cannot include any logos or branding other than those associated with the University; this even extended to colours of uniforms, flags, wall graphics, etc., so as not to be confused with the Olympic colours

- The Olympics cannot be mentioned or referred to, directly or indirectly

- The University wants to promote its assets and show its diversity of programs and depth of quality; a context of leadership is to be implied with restraint

- The University is the only educational institution advertising during the Olympic broadcast and wants to be perceived as being proud and confident, but not boastful (you have to love Canadian humility)

Step 2. The Idea String. List the content focusing on real evidence of the University's quality and leadership. Define the visuals and other elements (such as a potential voice or on-camera spokesperson) that speak for themselves.

- The University sports teams are highly accomplished, many of them champions in their category nationally

- The University shows strong leadership and innovation in science, business, engineering and arts

- There are several, well known alumni available in Edmonton where the commercial is to be shot

- The University's video archive is extensive and covers many aspects of the University's major programs; the University owns the footage

- The major facilities on campus are impressive visually

in terms of exterior and interior; signage is well positioned, making it highly visible and easy to read

- The University has not advertised on national television before, which means that the campus and the programs have not been seen nationally other than through regional and national broadcasts and coverage of major University sporting events

- Successful people do not talk about their successes; they remain quiet and unassuming with humility, letting others speak for them

Step 3. The Actionable Idea. My first instinct led me to the Actionable Idea almost instantly. Canadians are known for humility and self-deprecation. Canadian icons, like William Shatner, have wielded self-deprecation with artistic finesse. We have a lot to boast about, but we prefer to go about our business in an understated style. The idea was to use humility and self-deprecation in this television campaign to leverage the University's position; to boast without boasting, in fact, to boast about how we don't boast. Inherent in this idea was a strategy that would help position the University of Alberta within the commercial in a way that was less intrusive. This called for a reveal: talk about Canadians and, then, talk about the University.

The next step was to identify the spokesperson. This was critical to the success of the television commercial, because the viewer is unforgiving and subjective. They either like someone or don't like someone within the first six seconds.

We identified a University alumnus who was perfect

as the spokesperson and tested well with viewers. Vern Thiessen, an award winning playwright, had a look and style imbued with both academic and artistic characteristics. He was also well-spoken and articulate. His wry sense of humour reflected a certain, cool, attitude and he had a knack for delivering tongue-in-cheek messages effectively.

His almost casual, on-camera delivery in a stark, white studio was paired to strong, active, images of the University's programs. After each statement, a powerful visual would act as a dramatic counterpoint to its meaning. The produced, final script below won several awards north and south of the border. You can watch it on YouTube.

https://www.youtube.com/watch?v=UqKxiHSv25I

Studio: Vern Thiessen on camera	**Music:** Upbeat & driven **Vern:** As Canadians, we are quiet and unassuming.
Hockey Game: hard check against the boards; followed by: **Volleyball Game:** male player spikes ball over net	**Sound:** impact of hockey player against the board **Sound:** hard slap of volleyball being spiked
Studio: Vern Thiessen on camera	**Vern:** We don't take ourselves too seriously.
Science Lab: student focused intensely on research **School of Business Classroom:** lecturer addressing students	**Music:** continues
Studio: Vern Thiessen on camera	**Vern:** And we don't like to brag a lot.
Hockey Game: players celebrate a goal	**Sound:** hockey players cheering each other
Studio: Vern Thiessen on camera	**Vern:** Even though we have lots to brag about.
University Campus: front façade of campus building; university student wearing University of Alberta jacket walks into view	**Vern:** Take the University of Alberta in Edmonton.
Volleyball Game: female player serves ball; followed by: **Volleyball Game:** female players huddle **Title Over Visual:** Most National Championships in 10 years	**Sound:** slap of ball being served
Nanotechnology Lab: researchers in white suits **Title Over Visual:** Canada's Nanotechnology Research Centre	**Music:** continues
Electronics Lab: student watches arc of light climb between two conducting rods **Title Over Visual:** Most 3M National Teaching Awards	**Music:** continues, climaxes and stops when arc of light reaches top of conductors
Studio: Vern Thiessen on camera **Title Over Visual:** U of A Grad, Vern Thiessen, Governor General's Literary Award 2003	**Vern:** But, hey. If you got it, flaunt it.
Black Screen **Title In White Font:** Inspiring Great Achievement	**Sound Effect:** Stamping sound reinforces each word in title as it appears
Studio: Vern Thiessen on camera **Graphic:** University of Alberta logo **Title Over Visual:** www.ulaberta.ca	**Music:** closing stanza **Vern:** Go Canada.

CASE STUDY #13: *NIGHTINGALE CONANT*

Nightingale Conant in Chicago is a world leader in self improvement and has been in the success and motivational publishing industry since the early 60s. Many say they invented the industry. They are the world's largest producer of audio programs and the global leader in self-development education.

Founded by radio legend, Earl Nightingale, and direct marketing guru, Lloyd Conant, the company distributes the works of such motivational icons as Anthony Robbins, Zig Ziglar, Napoleon Hill, Dale Carnegie, Deepak Chopra, Seth Godin, Brian Tracy, Stephen Covey, Sylvia Browne, Denis Waitley, Wayne Dyer—it is a blue-chip list. It was the former CEO, Gary Chappell, who encouraged me to write this book.

Gary sought out a creative thinker on the web and contacted me out of the blue. He wanted to re-assess the company's brand and needed someone to work with his team. The reason he picked me? Instinct. A hunch. Over the course of four years, I led several think tank sessions and, together with his team, we explored the Nightingale Conant brand.

The objective of the process was to find a new slogan.

I love projects involving headlines, slogans, company and product names—anything involving succinct language including symbols and images. The first few creative sessions focused more on defining the company's essence, examining the vision and mission, which, for the most part, have remained unchanged for many decades.

With respect to employing Inherent Values, we more or less worked with all of them. The end result was simple and elegant. The last step we took to get to the slogan was one of the most extensive experiences in applying **Shitz & Giggles**.

Step 1. The Context. List the POVs around self-improvement and express them from the first person POV.

- I dream of success, but struggle with self-confidence and motivation
- I want to become a better decision maker
- I sabotage myself
- I am not creative
- I want financial security and the freedom to do the things I love
- I want better relationships
- I want to be more disciplined
- I need a change
- I want to manage my time better and become more productive

- I want to set clear objectives and achieve measureable results
- I want to improve the quality of my life

Step 2. The Idea String. As I mentioned previously, the Nightingale Conant team and I went through many steps. The last step was, perhaps, one of the most engaging exercises in creative process. Owing to its depth, the sub-steps are listed, rather than the language used.

- List as many words and phrases relating to the various contexts as possible; we listed hundreds of words and phrases on sticky notes and pasted them on every wall in the session room
- Reorganize all of the notes into categories and identify streams of thought
- Select notes that inspire the group and feel most relevant to the contexts listed
- Develop statements suggested or inspired by the filtered notes

Connect statements either by consolidating them into one statement or grouping statements in a relevant sequence

Fig. 10

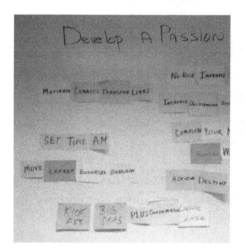

Fig. 11

Fig. 12

Step 3. The Actionable Idea. Two things became evident in the flow of discussion within the room. People dream and time is an issue. Time erodes dreams. The more we remain inactive, the more our dreams fade evanescently into the sunset like a shimmering bubble. Lastly, the burden of taking responsibility and taking action can be mitigated if we know there is a support structure; cheerleaders and coaches play an integral role in our self improvement.

Being a fan of the foundations of triptychs (3-panel pictures, often forming one cohesive image), I suggested we formulate a 3-statement slogan, a GPS of the brand, which would either be consolidated into one statement or left as is. The triptychs would include three contexts: dreams, time and support or action.

We went through various configurations until we arrived at the slogan now in use.

- It's your dream. It's time. Get started.
- It's your dream. It's your time. So, get started.
- It's your dream. It's your time. *Let's get started.*

As I said, simple and elegant—and relevant. The feeling was that the slogan had to be personalized. It also had to invoke a sense of action *and* support. The statement, "It's your time." had an inherent double-entendre; "your time" meant that it was your turn for success or that you earned the opportunity. It also implied that getting to your goal was a reflection of the time you would invest. The italicized *"Let's get started."* was deliberate: we take action together.

Summary. The acid test for some ad critics is to determine if a slogan can stand on its own. If a slogan is isolated in a vacuum, the meaning can be somewhat vague. For example, if you knew nothing about Nike, then the slogan, *"Just do it,"* would mean very little beyond the fact that it is a call to action. But, what action? An effective slogan or even the theme title for an event or program captures the essence and spirit of the brand and the connection the brand has to its audience or consumer. Marketing strategist, Don Norris, a colleague of mine with a wealth of international ad agency experience, sees branding this way: *"A brand is the space owned in the customer's mind. Your space will be small if your brand is not both different and relevant."*

CASE STUDY #14: *THIS & THAT—A COMPENDIUM*

In many respects, the development of slogans, themes, titles and headlines is an excellent starting point for any project, personal or professional. Another important exercise in establishing context (for anything) is to invest in the development of mission, value and vision statements. Having written and produced thousands of advertising campaigns, authoring articles and books, developing product concepts and learning how to communicate with four, very imaginative children, I have learned to appreciate the complexity within the simplicity of life's offerings. Most times, the less said, the better.

This case study is a short compendium of various statements, slogans, headlines, titles, promotions and concepts, which tell a story about finding ideas right in the open without requiring too much instinct or analysis. The **Context** has been stated as a simple objective. The **Idea String** is expressed as a creative strategy followed by the **Inherent Values** used to find the **Actionable Idea**, which is stated in its final form.

Step 1. The Context. Develop a slogan for a windshield repair provider.

Step 2. The Idea String. List words, turns of phrase and colloquialisms associated with the term "glass." **(Function-Result IVL, Cause-Effect IVL, By Implication IVL)**

Step 3. The Actionable Idea. *"The solution is as clear as glass."*

Step 1. The Context. Develop a slogan for an organic food association, understanding that organic food is not completely pure.

Step 2. The Idea String. List words, turns of phrase and colloquialisms associated with our connection to food. **(Function Result IVL, Cause-Effect IVL, By Implication IVL)**

Step 3. The Actionable Idea. *"There's more to love in our food."*

Step 1. The Context. Develop a brand name for a writing service.

Step 2. The Idea String. List words, turns of phrase and colloquialisms associated with writing; list the same using the context based on the word "right." **(By Implication IVL, Other Alternative IVL)**

Step 3. The Actionable Idea. *"The Write Service."*

Step 1. The Context. Develop a BBQ related slogan for a pork producers association.

Step 2. The Idea String. List words, turns of phrase and colloquialisms associated with our connection to food. **Function Result IVL, Cause-Effect IVL, By Implication IVL**

Step 3. The Actionable Idea. *"The thrill of the grill."*

Step 1. The Context. Develop a company name for a landscaping company.

Step 2. The Idea String. List words, turns of phrase and colloquialisms associated with landscaping and gardening. List words containing "scape." (**Function-Result IVL, Cause-Effect IVL, Negative Space Thinking IVL, By Implication IVL**)

Step 3. The Actionable Idea. *"Land Escape Artists."*

Step 1. The Context. Develop a name for an internet-based video network.

Step 2. The Idea String. List words, turns of phrase and colloquialisms associated with web-based streaming; list words specifically containing web-related expressions, such as "net." (**By Implication IVL, Attitude-Altitude IVL**)

Step 3. The Actionable Idea. *"InterNETional TV."*

Step 1. The Context. Develop a retail strategy involving extended warranties.

Step 2. The Idea String. List possible connections between the values of the products and the price-points of the extended warranties. (**Function-Result IVL, Cause-Effect IVL, Other Alternative IVL**)

Step 3. The Actionable Idea. After an extended warranty has expired, offer the same customer a discount on the next purchase equivalent to the value of the extended warranty. Either the purchase should be greater than the value of the extended warranty or, alternatively, the discount can be a smaller percentage of the extended warranty against the new purchase. Name the warranty, *"The Boomerang Warranty,"* because it comes back to the consumer.

Step 1. The Context. Develop a promotion for a retailer of a new, solar-powered, home energy system.

Step 2. The Idea String. List various aspects of home energy associated with home-owners as well as the impact of using solar-powered energy systems in the home. (**Function-Result IVL, Cause-Effect IVL, Other Alternative IVL, By Implication IVL, Proximity Influence IVL**)

Step 3. The Actionable Idea. Offer home-owners a free evaluation of their energy use and determine how much they will save in energy costs per month using the new solar-powered system. Offer a discount on the system based on the average monthly energy costs. (Example: discount may be based on 1-month, 2-months, or 3-months of savings.) Advertise the program on radio and sponsor the weather report. Print up flyers that look like local utility bills and distribute them in targeted, older neighbourhoods with less, energy-efficient homes. Call the program the *"Sunsational Savings Program"* and attach the byline, *"Rays Your Home's Energy Efficiency."*

Step 1. The Context. Write a memorable radio commercial for a weight loss company, Nutrisystem.

Step 2. The Idea String. List positive and negative issues and practices relating to weight loss. **(Problem-Solution IVL, Cause-Effect IVL, By Implication IVL, Negative Space Thinking IVL)**

Step 3. The Actionable Idea. The final commercial won an award in Hollywood and was honoured as one of the World's Best Broadcast Advertisements. The first 15 seconds was the reason why.

Imagine a repetitive *boinging* sound accompanied by a voice humming mindlessly and intermittently. No words; just *boinging* and *humming*. After 15 seconds, a gentle, wry voiceover intrudes with a simple statement, *"Losing weight doesn't have to be a rubber room experience."* The remainder of the commercial was a simple call to action directing the listener to try Nutrisystem's program and products.

Step 1. The Context. Develop a story concept for a film about artists with disabilities.

Step 2. The Idea String. List disabilities and then pair them up. (**By Implication IVL, Negative Space Thinking IVL**)

Step 3. The Actionable Idea. *"A blind musician meets a deaf painter and they fall in love."*

Step 1. The Context. Develop a retail sale name for a New Year's promotion.

Step 2. The Idea String. List words, turns of phrase and colloquialisms associated with New Year's. (**By Implication IVL**)

Step 3. The Actionable Idea. *"The Hung Over Sale."* Write ad copy to include the statement, *"This sale has been hung over, I mean, held over."*

Step 1. The Context. Develop a TV commercial concept for an agency providing services to immigrants and refugees.

Step 2. The Idea String. List the issues and challenges faced by immigrants and refugees learning to adapt to a new culture and lifestyle. (**Problem-Solution IVL, Cause-Effect IVL, Negative Space Thinking IVL, By Implication IVL**)

Step 3. The Actionable Idea. Tell four stories of

immigrants and refugees on screen at the same time. Develop complex, tension filled scenes and dialogues about issues immigrants and refugees face in adapting to a new life, such as applying for a job, shopping in a store, and trying to get information about a school over the phone.

Show these scenes simultaneously in four split screens, deliberately allowing the dialogues and actions to become confusing to the viewer, but still allowing the viewers to catch pieces of the verbal exchanges, enough to understand the contexts.

Each scene's tension escalates until they all come to an abrupt stop. Following the climax, the visuals cut to a close-up of the four key individuals looking strained, tired, frustrated and helpless. After a brief silent pause, we hear a voice saying, *"If you think you're confused, imagine what they're going through."* This is followed by a scene showing one of the individuals consulting with a representative from the agency.

Step 1. The Context. Develop a radio promotion to promote international sales of the Canadian National Best Selling Book, *"The Bachelor's Guide to Ward off Starvation,"* a simple, throw-the-leaves-in-a-bowl, recipe book.

Step 2. The Idea String. List dates throughout the year that are associated with gift giving to men. **(Proximity Influence IVL, Function-Result IVL)**

Step 3. The Actionable Idea. The most obvious time to run a promotion for this type of publication was in the two weeks leading into Father's Day. Unfortunately, the publisher did not allocate any funds to buy radio, so the challenge was to convince radio stations in Canada, the US, Australia and England to talk about the book without charging us for the airtime.

We proposed the following to the stations. We offered them 10 copies of the book and asked them to give them away during a one-week period prior to Father's Day, once in morning drive time and once in afternoon drive (their peak listening times). They could do anything they liked as long as they directed listeners to the book's website.

The request was made through emails targeting program managers and promotions managers. If we couldn't find those contacts, we targeted morning and afternoon radio show hosts. About 100 radio stations in four countries jumped on board. For the cost of 1000 books plus shipping (around $15,000), we received approximately $250,000 to $300,000 in radio advertising exposure. Online sales of the books were brisk and we expanded the promotion to include the Christmas season.

Step 1. The Context. Develop an outdoor billboard advertising concept for a mattress manufacturer and retailer.

Step 2. The Idea String. List images associated with beds. Include cartoon images focused on the topic of sleep. (**Function-Result IVL**)

Step 3. The Actionable Idea. One of the most popular images I found showed a foot sticking out of the end of the bed. I suggested to the creative designer at the billboard company that he create the image of a foot sticking out of the end of a bed, exaggerating the big toe. I also asked them to design a mechanical big toe that would not only protrude beyond the borders of the billboard, but would also wiggle back and forth non-stop.

It was a costly proposition, so the retailer limited himself to one super-sized billboard and moved it around the city over a period of months. The final product received significant attention and won an advertising award.

––––––––––––––––––––––

Step 1. The Context. Develop an alternative marketing strategy for a weekly, classifieds publication.

Step 2. The Idea String. Examine all the topic areas in the publication to determine where the opportunities are to develop alternative marketing strategies. Assess the current advertising program and identify gaps in the communication plan. (**Function-Result IVL, Proximity Influence IVL**)

Step 3. The Actionable Idea. The publication had one section devoted to garage sales. The listings were extensive. It occurred to me that most people made their own garage sale signs, but some people did source pre-made signs from the major newspaper in the city. I also realized that these small signs, peppered throughout the neighbourhoods, were a very active form of outdoor advertising. So, I suggested to the publisher that he create a garage sale package, which included signs, price stickers and inventory sheets. The program was an immediate success and led to increased circulation of the publication.

CASE STUDY #15: *YOUR CASE STUDY*

Step 1. The Context. What do you need an idea for? Describe your passion, your dream or your situation. What do you understand about it now? State what you know about what you don't know.

_____

_____

_____

Step 2. The Idea String. Pick one of the **Inherent Values** that you feel suits your case best: Function-Result, Cause-Effect, Problem-Solution, By Implication, Negative Space Thinking, The Other Alternative, Proximity Influence, Attitude-Altitude, Shitz & Giggles. Alternatively, just pick one and start from there. Allow yourself to drift, shift and change lanes whenever you want. Create lists based on language and images. Examine connections between them. Remember to pay attention to your hunches and instincts.

_____

_____

_____

Step 3. The Actionable Idea. Life is about to get interesting.

_____

_____

_____

CHAPTER 12.

AND SO WE CARRY ON . . .

If we were to be able to capture the absolute moment of existence, a singularity that may well be the unifying factor, we might be able to realize that on either side of that moment are two other moments creating a symmetry within an interminable balancing act that invokes reality, moment to moment. All we ever know is the one moment in the middle. This is the present, to which we give meaning. This is how we give definition to life. As such, perfection is imperfection at work.
—Michael Kryton

Every moment we live and breathe, we create life. Surviving is how we sustain ourselves; but, life is more than survival. Thousands of ideas shape our individual and collective destinies every second. We invoke and innovate, create and destroy, wandering through a landscape filled with the relics of our intentions.

We hope and dream for something better. Some of us want to give up. Many of us don't think we have the capability to realize the things we think about. It took me 6 years to get to these words, sometimes driven only by faith in what I didn't know would become reality with any certainty—except for one thing. I believe we are all creative and filled with brilliant ideas. They live within us, in our experience, knowledge and instincts, fueled by passion and dreams. Anything is possible. The alternative means nothing.

I encourage you to keep searching for ideas with the hope that what I have provided is tangible in its application. Never underestimate any idea. And never underestimate your ability or the ability of those around you to generate ideas.

Henry Ford, inventor of the assembly line that changed the world, said. *"The air is full of ideas. They are knocking you in the head all the time. You only have to know what you want, then forget it, and go about your business. Suddenly, the idea will come through. It was there all the time."*

Perhaps one day we will meet, either face to face, or within an exchange of words, spoken or read, through the myriad channels of communication at our disposal. I ask you to share your ideas with me because it will contribute to my learning and it will expand the vastness of my own ignorance.

I've always appreciated Mahatma Gandhi's statement, *"Be the change you wish to see in the world."* He believed in the good of humanity and held to simple ideas: freedom, peace and happiness. This one, humble and determined man could not change the world on his own; but his idea that the world could change for the better, an idea that was, for him, irrefutable, inspired millions to act. Millions of people, together, manifested change.

Likewise, a half million people landed one human being on the moon; over a billion and a half people (and counting) adopted a worldwide, online network, creating a new community; thousands of scientists and doctors keep searching for cures for diseases threatening our existence; many more are reaching for new worlds deep in the ocean, within the particles and elements that hold the tenuous fabric of our physical reality together, and out in the silence of space, seeking clues to the secrets of who we are, trying to determine if we are not alone.

We are always questing for answers, digging through the questions that may unlock the mysteries, which drive our insatiable curiosity. Shakespeare was far more eloquent in describing our sense of wonder. *"There are more things in heaven and earth, Horatio, Than are dreamt of in your philosophy."* (Hamlet, 1.5.167–8, Hamlet to Horatio)

We create change through ideas. It only takes one idea. You have, at least, one brilliant idea inside you. Find it. And then, find another one. And another one—every 60 seconds.

And so, we carry on . . .

Your turn.
What do you need an idea for?

Go!

ABOUT THE AUTHOR

Michael Kryton has the unique ability to bring out the creative genius inside us. His learnable techniques spawn inspired solutions and can be tapped any time. Absolutely brilliant!
—Gary Chappell, Past President/CEO, Nightingale-Conant; CEO, Chappell Enterprises

Michael Kryton is an Ideation Expert who has been generating ideas and concepts for over 35 years. As an international, award winning writer and producer, his creative experience spans radio, television, print, web, live shows and events. His work has been recognized in New York, Hollywood, and Toronto.

He has handled creative assignments for many organizations in the public and private sectors, generating ideas with teams for many different applications spanning advertising and marketing ideas and concepts to problem solving and strategic solutions The list of projects is diverse including branding development for Nightingale Conant in Chicago, to co-scripting and directing William Shatner's live Canadian show. He is also the author of *"The Father's Guide To Surviving With Kids,"* the third installment for the Bachelor's Guide Series, which has collectively sold over 300,000 copies in Canada.

|*A Brilliant Idea Every 60 Seconds* and the related workshop apply to all: entrepreneurs, marketers, advertisers, educators, students, professionals, writers, communicators, non-profit, industry teams, artists, scientists, researchers, inventors—anyone who needs an idea. It is a multi-platform toolkit for ideation and creative thinking.

Reach out to him on LinkedIn/Facebook as well as MichaelKryton.com, @MichaelKryton, SKYPE Michael.Kryton.

Printed in the USA
CPSIA information can be obtained
at www.ICGtesting.com
JSHW012022140824
68134JS00033B/2822